YOU'VE GOT TO TELL THEM

Ida Grinspan, at twelve years old, before her deportation to Auschwitz

A French Girl's Experience of Auschwitz and After

YOU'VE GOT TO TELL THEM

IDA GRINSPAN *and*
BERTRAND POIROT-DELPECH

Translated by Charles B. Potter

LOUISIANA STATE UNIVERSITY PRESS BATON ROUGE

Publication of this English-language edition is made possible by an anonymous donation made through the Baton Rouge Area Foundation

Manufactured in the United States of America
First printing

Frontispiece courtesy Ida Grinspan.

Designer: Barbara Neely Bourgoyne
Typeface: Fournier Pro
Printer and binder: Sheridan Books

LIBRARY OF CONGRESS CATALOGING-IN-PUBLICATION DATA
Names: Grinspan, Ida, 1929– author. | Poirot-Delpech, Bertrand, author.
Title: You've got to tell them : a French girl's experience of Auschwitz and after / Ida Grinspan and Bertrand Poirot-Delpech ; translated by Charles B. Potter.
Other titles: J'ai pas pleur?e. English
Description: Baton Rouge : Louisiana State University Press, 2018. | "Copyright 2002 by ?Editions Robert Laffont; preface and afterword copyright 2003 by ?Editions Pocket Jeunesse, d?epartement d'Univers Poche." | Includes bibliographical references.
Identifiers: LCCN 2018001498| ISBN 9780807169803 (cloth : alk. paper) | ISBN 9780807169797 (pdf) | ISBN 9780807169810 (epub)
Subjects: LCSH: Grinspan, Ida, 1929—Childhood and youth. | Jewish children in the Holocaust—France—Biography. | Holocaust, Jewish (1939–1945)—France—Personal narratives. | Auschwitz (Concentration camp)
Classification: LCC DS135.F9 G7513 2018 | DDC 940.53/18092 [B]—dc23
LC record available at https://lccn.loc.gov/2018001498

The paper in this book meets the guidelines for permanence and durability of the Committee on Production Guidelines for Book Longevity of the Council on Library Resources. ∞

For my parents
murdered at Auschwitz

For my daughter Sophie

IDA

The secret of Hope
is the secret of brotherhood.

—GENEVIÈVE DE GAULLE-ANTHONIOZ

CONTENTS

FRENCH PUBLISHER'S PREFACE

Fourteen years old, still a child, already an adolescent. Ida is in hiding deep in the Poitou countryside.[1] The war is not over in the opening days of 1944, but the news is good. Ida can allow herself to hope that she will slip through the net.

Then comes her arrest by the French police, suddenly and unprovoked. Auschwitz, two endless winters. The struggle for survival, with glimmers of hope in the depths of hell.

Impossible to say the unspeakable with words. *You Have to Tell Them*, beyond being the account of one person's experience, continually asks the same question: How could human beings, German soldiers, French police, act as accomplices, out of fear or out of blindness, of the killing machine that the Nazi regime had become?

How to survive the camp, how to have the strength to bear witness to what happened there, how to overcome the urge to forget in order to fulfill the "sacred mission" bestowed upon Ida by her companions on the road to death:

"If you get back, you've got to tell them. They won't believe you, but you've got to tell them."

FOREWORD

We met in March 1988, at Auschwitz. It was the first time that Ida had returned to the camp since her liberation in 1945. She made herself do it in order to be able to testify to a class of high school students from the Paris region. Bertrand had joined the travel group, which he was going to write about in *Le Monde.*[1]

We saw each other again often, during ceremonies or gatherings connected with memory. In April 2001, news received from the Polish nurse who had saved Ida's life in the infirmary at Neustadt brought us a little closer together. "Wanda is alive!" Ida called to say. Bertrand immediately remembered this name that Ida had mentioned several times during her 1988 visit to the camp. As Fate had it, only a few hours kept the former girl with frozen feet from seeing once again the woman who saved her life: Wanda Ossowska died in Warsaw at the age of eighty-nine.

This missed rendezvous with reconnection reminded Ida how time works to thwart memory. At age seventy-two, wasn't it time to put down in black on white the testimony that she had been scattering in front of classes of school kids, lest all that remained were vanishing traces? She was perfectly capable of setting down her memories, she whom Madame Picard, her teacher from the Deux-Sèvres,[2] considered—as we shall soon see—as her best student in French. But she would feel less intimidated by the writing of it if only . . .

Bertrand volunteered to be the scribe of this work for four hands that Nicole Lattès decided to publish at Robert Laffont. The deal was sealed in 2001, with the intense serenity that such shared conceptions inspire. The story would be Ida's, it would have her face, her voice, as she had indeed lived it in the flesh. Bertrand would have the role of narrator, to recall contemporary events, and to express those things that emotion or humility might prevent Ida from stating on her own.

Thanks to being born French Catholics, neither Bertrand nor his family had had to suffer directly from the war waged by the Nazis and their accomplices on a little Jewish girl of fourteen, all the way to the distant reaches of a farm in the Poitou. He had felt something akin to scandal and shame over his sheltered adolescence when a friend, Youra Riskin, disappeared from his class in school in June of 1943; and then there were the trials of the Shoah—Barbie, Touvier, and Papon[3]—which he had followed in the hope of better understanding, of honoring, of transmitting.

What you are about to read had the strange effect of uniting us as brother and sister. We were both born in 1929! Let us say that this coincidence worked out well for us, while at the same time not wanting to make too much of a connection that arises, like the subject of our mingled sentences, from the unspeakable.

IDA AND BERTRAND

YOU'VE GOT TO TELL THEM

PART I

“The Jewess of Lié”

The Sound of a Motor in the Night

It is after midnight, January 31, 1944, when a Traction Avant[1] pulls up next to the farmhouse of the Marché family, at Jeune-Lié, not far from Melle,[2] in Poitou. Behind the solid wall, a young girl wakes up suddenly. None of the neighbors would be venturing out to this place at such an hour.

"It can only be for me!" fourteen-year-old Ida Fensterzab says to herself, not yet realizing that she has just entered the point of focus of one of the greatest outrages in human history . . .

A victorious army, though on the point of being beaten, that still can find nothing more urgent to do than to press its subjects to go and round up a little Jewish girl from the Deux-Sèvres in order to send her to hell in Auschwitz! The Homeland of the Arts waging a war to the death against a child, among thousands of others, for the crime of simply having been born! . . . The circumstance is so atrocious, so unimaginable, that one ends up not imagining it at all, no lightning bolts from the sky, no Wagnerian racket, without even a chorus of mourners.

But barbarity enters on tiptoes—Ida's first lesson from what she will live through—on this winter night, in a hamlet where everything seemed to promise the peaceful slumber of places forgotten by History. It is through the random chance of thwarted precaution that supreme inhumanity thrust its head in, behind the faces of policemen whom one wants to believe to be good and pious fathers, despite their staggering lack of any spontaneous sense of pity, and without showing any other sign of the monstrousness of what they were up to—for they did let on that they knew what the future held in store—than a big checkered bandana pulled out to wipe a sweating brow, as a sign of embarrassment. Thus tragedies are born quietly, on the sly: when will we understand that? Always too late?

Ida's tragedy is intricately woven, as always when evil stalks the innocent, out of an accretion of tiny gestures, of many little lucky or unlucky events. It would be enough to make one superstitious, if it didn't ultimately reveal that some very stubborn logic was in fact at work.

France, the Place of Refuge

In the overheated car where the horror begins, Ida will say nothing, her hand resting on her bundle. The cop who is mopping his uneasy brow doesn't deserve to know what faith in his country had drawn the Fensterzabs to France, with the result that their daughter had now fallen into the paws of the "squad" from Melle. He would only become even redder in the face.

Now a half-century has passed, and the offspring of the good soldier have the right—some would even say the obligation—to hear the epic of these Polish Jews whose only true country was exile. This epic is one of betrayed trust. Let's listen to it in one go, from Ida's mouth—while on her arm one can still make out the identification number that was tattooed on her upon arrival in Auschwitz (this part of the interview is taking place on a beautiful summer day in Normandy,[3] in July of 2001). The number is 75,360, and in it her executioners saw clear proof of abject servility. In time it has become a powerful symbol of victory over Nothingness.

"My mother was from Ostrów-Mazowiecka, not far from Warsaw.[4] My father was from Koprzywnica,[5] further to the east. I haven't ever visited these cradles of my family. I have only become acquainted with Auschwitz out of necessity, and with the capital. My maternal grandfather was a forest and river warden. My mother, as was not uncommon for women of her generation, did not go to school for very long. Her parents died in the world war of 1914. She worked as an equipment operator in the fur industry. Around 1921 she moved to Berlin where she lived with an uncle.

"It was there that she met my father, who had arrived from his part of Poland. They had a religious wedding in Berlin, followed by a civil wedding in Paris, in the City Hall of the 11th *arrondissement*,[6] after getting all of the necessary documents together, in 1926. My brother was already born (in 1924). I was born five years later, in 1929.

"My father's name, Fensterzab, means 'window pane,' probably from some ancestor's being a glazier. My father wasn't able to stay in school for very long either. His father died when he was young and there were five kids to feed. He began working at age fourteen, as a tailor. Because of his own difficult childhood he developed a true reverence for school, and he considered attendance to be a privilege. He had very high expectations regarding our grades. The language used around the house was Yiddish, an old German dialect from the Rhineland that the Jews then spread over all of central Europe.

"Later, my father took French lessons, and he would ask me for advice, which I found truly admirable. He didn't want me to come to his classes. They took place on Sunday mornings. Often he tried to catch me on a question of conjugation, and he was proud when he succeeded. He filled entire exercise books with French lessons. I found them in 1945. Alas, I have no idea what became of them . . .

"My parents were married in a religious ceremony. They didn't have the necessary papers for a civil wedding, but except for the occasional high holiday, they were not observant at all. They didn't invoke God, but Man, and the Republic. They taught a very strict moral code: what you should do, what you should not do.

"Poland was victim to a deeply felt anti-Semitism. I learned what the word *pogrom*[7] meant very early in life. My father told me about them. Since he worked at home—while my mother made the deliveries in town—he talked to us a lot. The years before 1940 were very important for me thanks to these conversations. Being born in 1898, my father was both a witness and a victim of these pogroms, in that part of the country which was annexed by the Russians before 1914. Mobs would spring up out of nowhere in towns or villages to pillage, rape, and massacre the

Jewish population. They could do anything they wanted. The police didn't try to stop them.

"In addition to the pogroms, there was a general discrimination practiced by the Poles. Jews were not considered full-fledged citizens. There were quotas on how many could enroll for school. My father never stopped stressing how lucky we were to be admitted without any conditions whatsoever.

"Aside from the anti-Semitism, it was the economic situation and inflation in the 1920s that forced them to leave Poland and then Berlin, where they had been happier. It should be noted that, having been born in Paris, my brother and I obtained French citizenship merely by the voluntary declaration of our parents, while they never got it themselves. Our final destination was supposed to be Canada, where some of our uncles had emigrated at the end of the 19th century. But my father did not want to go there without us, as a scout. Paris seemed a safe enough place to be.

"France had an incredible reputation in central Europe at the time. Without actually knowing anyone there, they knew that France had made the Revolution, it was the land of liberty, of tolerance, the country that had freed its Jews. When war was declared, my father volunteered immediately as a foreigner. If he didn't serve it was, I believe, because he was judged to be too old—over forty years old. Even when the Vichy regime came to power, we refused to believe that it would be a threat to us. France had a prodigious aura about it, nothing could touch it!

"At first we lived in the 11th *arrondissement,* rue de Montreuil, then rue des Envierges in the 20th. After 1935 we had a very nice apartment with four bedrooms, rue Clavel, in the 19th. I lived there when I returned from the camps. Since then, the individual houses have been demolished and a big apartment house built in their place.

"My memories start at around age four, around 1933, at the kindergarten of the 20th *arrondissement.* I learned French, which I hardly could speak at all. I got it mixed up with the Yiddish that was spoken at home. At the Hauser dairy products store I might ask for *keisele,* instead of cheese. The saleswoman corrected me very kindly. The racism common in the press, and in the bourgeois intellectual world in general at the time, is not felt in the local schools in the neighborhood where most of the Jewish families live.

"Amongst the emigré population, we see a lot of each other. They are all Ashkenazies like us and they speak Yiddish. My parents worked very hard. As soon as dinner was done, we would clear the table off and work would continue, work sewing, by hand and not by machine, so as not to disturb the neighbors. My Uncle and my Aunt Dembski lived in Clamart,[8] in the Paris suburbs. We had fun bathing together. My father was a riot. He enjoyed tall tales, jokes in Yiddish, which is a very rich language. Among our neighbors there was an Armenian tailor (from whom I heard very young in life about the massacres in his country), an Italian bootmaker, and the keeper of the bar on the ground floor that served as a telephone booth. My parents enjoyed very close friendships with all of the neighbors. Alas, many of their friends were deported never to return, often as early as 1942.[9]

"News comes from Germany all the time, via refugees coming from Berlin and elsewhere. From 1937 or '38 onward we are aware of what is happening to the Jews across the Rhine. Everyone is talking about it. We are worried about it. Although we have no radio at home, I can recall seeing my parents listening to a speech of Hitler at the home of friends. They understood German from the time they had spent in Berlin. Myself, I did not catch the meaning of what the Führer was screaming. But the anxiety it produced in the grown-ups was certainly felt by the children.

"My father read a leftist newspaper, in Yiddish, the *Neue Presse,* which I went to get from the neighboring stationery shop. The Russian Revolution of 1917 was an important point of reference at the time. I remember very clearly a parade of the Popular Front,[10] in a large square, la Nation or la République, I can't say which. I was on my father's shoulders. I remember my surprise: why was everyone singing about '*serviettes* everywhere'?[11] My father set me straight right away: "'the Soviets, Ida, the Soviets, like in the U.S.S.R.!'"

While everything separated Ida and Bertrand as children with regard to both the comforts and the risks involved in life, Bertrand recalls having a similar exchange with his father, in 1938, involving the Danzig corridor in Poland, which he confused with "dancing." "Surely they aren't going to war over 'dancing,'" he protested. Proof that living through the same events at the same time creates a secret bond, no matter how far apart people are born. There is a commonality between everybody born in the same generation, a homeland without borders.

Popular entertainment of the day is also a part of the riches shared by the alumni of the 1930s. So it is with the Walt Disney cartoon *Snow White*, in theaters around 1937, or the operetta *Yana*, at the Châtelet.[12] Ida has only good memories of going out with her family:

"My parents took me with them. We went to plays in Yiddish in the rue de Lancry. On the boulevard de Belleville there were films in Yiddish. I knew the language quite well, and since it is close to German this would be a help to me in the camp, it saved me. . . . We also went for walks and picnics in the forest of Vincennes.[13] And we often visited with friends.

"In school, I was never made to feel that I was from somewhere else, neither by the teachers or by the other students. Nobody joked about my name, which was admittedly difficult to pronounce, except for Madame S., who was not very nice.[14] On the other hand my first grade teacher, who taught me how to read, Madame Roubéda, was especially nice, sweet and motherly. I tried to find her after the war, without success."

Country Girl

In fact, Ida knew nothing directly about the increasing danger to Jewish immigrants living in eastern Paris during the Occupation, and this for the very good reason that her parents sent her to the countryside even before the massive departure of the civilian population in June of 1940. This decision was not made out of fear of persecution but to protect her from bombardments, invasion, and expected shortages. She had already arrived in the Deux-Sèvres region in 1939 where she met up with her Uncle and Aunt Dembski along with her mother and brother. So it was that she arrived in the home of Alice in Jeune-Lié, near Melle, some 30 kilometers from Niort.[15]

We went there together—for Bertrand to get to know the place, for Ida to see it again and to serve as a guide—aided by the kindness and erudition of a man who was a top specialist in local history, Jean-Marie Pouplain, a correspondent of the Institute for History of the Present Time.[16] Later we will tell the story of the emotion we all felt during our meeting with Madame Picard, Ida's former school teacher in the nearby village of Sompt. The most striking revelation of the trip was Ida's ease, her almost physical attachment to this land of which she made herself, as it were, the proud representative. Illustrating her account of daily life with expressions in the local dialect, she spoke of "her" school, of "her" road, of "her" sheep, about "her" dog Gardienne, of the relationships of the people buried in "her" cemetery in Sompt.

The village had done more than adopt her: it had instantly erased the differences that might have existed because of where she came from, and of the situation in which she found herself. This perfect immersion in the landscape and the population would add to the humiliation of the anti-Jewish measures taken by the Vichy government starting in October 1940, even before the Nazi occupiers required them, and of the arrest by French men of this "child of the country"!

You have to imagine the hamlet of Jeune Lié: a cluster of houses in light-colored stone whose poor, hardscrabble look has been well preserved by the general depression of the countryside. Few windows, an enclosed courtyard, a very present smell of liquid manure, a few acres of mixed culture farming, some animal husbandry, a few goats and a few sheep, a chicken coop, a strong attachment to Catholicism, the harmony of roosters and bells wafted on a sea breeze, the Poitevin swamp just around the corner, changeable weather: a frugal way of life, friendly, with a skillfully crafted artisanal balance to it, very little-known despite the hymns that the local poet Pierre Moinot dedicated to it.[17]

Ida wasted no time getting back to school. She enrolled in the spring of 1940. She was just about ready to take the *certificat d'études*, which she would pass with ease in the following year. In her spare time she keeps sheep, who become her confidants on days when she is lonely. Alice, who has no children, takes her boarder in completely. In her school in Sompt, Ida makes friends right away. Life is in full bloom. All that is missing is the warmth of a real family.

The German army arrives on the scene. In Lié, this doesn't have quite the same shocking effect as in Paris. When her mother comes to visit in 1941 she tells Ida about how the soldiers of the Reich entered the capital via the Porte des Lilas and the rue de Belleville, the fear, the grief. The arrival of the Wehrmacht[18] along the road outside the Marché farm several days later is more bucolic, less offensive. The soldiers watered their horses in the pond down at the corner, which has been drained since then. They must have toppled the French forces very fast to get so far at the speed of horse-drawn equipment!

Following which the occupier's weight on the land is hardly felt, it feels a bit distant. Except for the requisition of all bicycles owned by Jews, by order of the German authorities. In 1942 Ida had to turn over the bike that was so useful to her given the distances between Lié and her school in Sompt or to Melle. She feels the persecution mainly through the bad news in letters from her father, who is hiding out in the Paris region. It will become a harsh reality and a direct threat when in the summer of '42 her father informs her of the arrest of her mother in the roundup of the Vel' d'Hiv'.[19]

Another date that mattered a lot to Ida was Spring Break at Easter of 1941, when her mother came and spent three or four days in the Deux-Sèvres region. Ida remembers every detail:

"Mother slept with me, in the house belonging to Alice, who had not yet remarried—she didn't marry Paul until 1943. I remember this in particular because Alice invited us both to attend Mass at the chapel in Sompt with her on Easter Sunday. My mother accepted with pleasure. I think we went in a horse-drawn cart that we borrowed from a neighbor. I was so proud to show off my mother to my girlfriends. Mother was beautiful, with her fair complexion and her frank way of looking at the world. She had made herself a cute little hat; so much so that the Englishwoman living in the village asked her to make her one!

"Something important happened," Ida adds about this visit. A day when Ida had annoyed her a bit, undoubtedly. "Alice had made several remarks, not in a mean way at all, but very sure of herself. According to her, 'It was the Jews who had killed Christ.' The old anti-Semitic story of the Catholic Church about the 'Jewish deicide' had not passed the remote Poitevin countryside by!

"It had taken me completely by surprise. We never talked about it when I was growing up. I always knew that I was Jewish, but I did not know this story about how the Jews had 'assassinated Christ.' I was saddened by it, and I felt guilty. 'Are you sure?' I asked Alice. She said that it was a certainty, it was a part of the catechism, it was even in one of the Psalms. For her, no doubt at all: Judas had betrayed, and we the Jews, my ancestors, we had 'killed Jesus.' I took advantage of my mother's visit to ask her about it when Alice wasn't around. She explained very calmly that it wasn't the Jews but the Romans who had killed Christ, and that first off, to begin with, Jesus himself was Jewish. This definitely took me by complete surprise. My mother went on to say that Jesus was an illegitimate child, born out of wedlock, and that Christianity arose out of this story. I kept all of this to myself, I never spoke to Alice about it again, but I was reassured.

"To keep me occupied, Alice sent me into the fields to take care of the sheep, with the help of a little dog named Gardienne. When I was sad and crying, thinking about my mother whom I soon had no news of, Gardienne consoled me by licking my face and whimpering, as if to say that she shared my sorrow. You will hear later on what an affectionate response Gardienne saved up for me when I returned, following the war.

"Alice often got upset with me because of the packages I sent to my parents every week. She raged: "I won't get any thanks for doing it anyway. . . . Everybody knows that the Jews are ungrateful!"

How to explain this curious mix of generous sentiments, in Alice, along with persistent prejudices that were the result of her education? Ida has an idea about this:

"It has to be said that Alice was no longer the same following the arrest of my mother. My father could no longer work as much, because he had to live in hiding. He survived by doing alterations. Alice no longer received payments for my board as regularly as before. She was now remarried and the mood was changing. She went away for six months to take a knitting apprenticeship in Melle. Her new husband was not unkind to me, no, but he was slightly jealous of the place that I took up."

Did Ida's mother express concern over the situation?

"If so, she didn't reveal it to me. But a neighbor told me fifty years later that my mother had seemed sad, anxious and preoccupied, during her visit in 1941. To me she seemed to be harping on the same things that all mothers of precocious twelve-year-old girls did: be wary of boys, do not trust them."

The last time that Ida saw her mother was in 1942. Ida spent the Easter vacation in Paris. She does not recall witnessing the bullying of Jews that was happening by this time, the signs placed on Jewish businesses. Since wearing the yellow star was not yet a requirement, she didn't hesitate to go out to the movies with her girlfriends. She saw *Romance de Paris* and *Allô, Janine!*. It was during this visit that her mother took her to a hairdresser's and got her the famous "*houpette*" hair-do that would make her seem older than she really was. Another scene that she recalls: the mother of some friends of hers expresses surprise in front of her, in a "tight-lipped way," that her mother is planning to let her return to the countryside. As far as she was concerned, she could never be apart from her children. Ida, who would just as happily have stayed in Paris, asked her mother to explain why she had to go back. Her mother had her answer ready, and it didn't mention the risk of being arrested which justified her attitude.

"Well, as for me, I love you even more than that lady loves her kids," she said to me. "Too bad if I am not with you, I prefer that you be in the countryside where you are well provided for."

Doubtless she guessed Alice's prejudices. She went so far as to get Ida to promise that "after the war" she would not remain in the countryside, that she would return to Paris to finish her studies. Ida remembered this when she returned from the camps. But at the time, separation seemed the only way to be safe. If her parents hadn't insisted on sending her back to Lié, Ida would have turned up on the lists for Paris. . . . And she would not have returned!

Once back in the Deux-Sèvres, Ida wrote what would be her last letter to her mother, telling her in guarded terms, out of respect for her father and brother, that the signs of puberty that they had discussed had appeared.

"So Mother had time to learn that I had become a young woman! If she hadn't warned me what was going to happen, I would have gone crazy! It provided me some kind of inner calm, it still does, to know that before she left, my mother learned that I had become a big person!"

Mrs. Fensterzab was arrested several days after she received this news. She would carry this knowledge into the great unknown.

"You Will Never See Her Again!"

"You are asleep when the car pulls up in the road, on the night of January 30, 1944?"

"Sure! In the winter, it gets dark early. Everyone is in bed by 10 p.m."

"How do you spend the evenings?"

"We shuck corn, we would go visit the neighbors. Everyone would get together and sit up. There was a very convivial atmosphere. I was very happy then. Or else I would read, I stayed home with Alice and her husband."

"You spoke the local dialect?"

"I knew it, but mainly I had a very strong accent in French. In the camp, later on, the other girls asked me where I got an accent like that. . . ."

"Your room was heated?"

"Yes, by a wood stove. I helped put wood in it, and I cleaned out the ashes."

"Did Alice come and kiss you and tuck you in?"

"No. We kissed before that. Afterwards I was all alone with my thoughts. One falls asleep quickly in the country."

"You didn't have homework to do after dinner?"

"From way back! After I passed the *Certificat,* in 1941, the teacher in Sompt, Madame Picard, made me work for a year, and after that I did an apprenticeship at the knitting mill in Melle that lasted about six months. During the day preceding my arrest I think I might have taken the sheep for a walk. I didn't operate the knitting machine that someone had lent me because it was Sunday. . . ."

"When the sound of the automobile wakes you up, you have often said that you told yourself immediately: 'It's undoubtedly for me!'"

"That's true. It was absolutely clear to me."

"Why was that? What news had you heard from outside?"

"Alice didn't have a radio. Her husband read a small-town newspaper from Melle that was censored by the Germans. The neighbors had a radio and they told us things. I didn't even know that there was radio from England, that there had been an Appeal of 18 June.[20] There were no Germans in Sompt. They only showed up to purchase food at the local farms. In Melle we would see them marching. I remember the sound of their boots. But we were as yet unaware what they were capable of. They sped by in cars. It was the speed that impressed us the most. We were unaware of any confrontations with local resistance groups, which they later used as an excuse for arresting the Jews."

"Your certainty that this nighttime visit had to be for you, where did that come from?"

"For a while my father had been writing to Alice urging her insistently to get my name taken off the rolls at the Town Hall, that it was really dangerous, that I should not even have a food ration card. The mayor, whom Alice had told this to, wasn't worried in the slightest. 'If it's risky,' he said, 'I know the chief of the local unit of the *gendarmerie*,[21] and he will warn me.' As a result of which Alice did not get my name removed from the lists, even though I would have gotten along fine without tickets, we never lacked for anything in the countryside. I was not old enough and didn't have the authority to insist that they follow my father's instructions."

"What other signs had you seen that made you worry when you heard this car?"

"I had officially been given the regulation yellow stars in 1942. The mayor, Monsieur Poupinot, had called me in to the Town Hall. He handed me three stars, saying, 'Here's what came for you! You have to sign to acknowledge that you received them, but as long as I am mayor, you will not wear them!' So I never wore the star publicly. But to be on the safe side I had sewed it onto my clothes in case there was a spot check."

"In the village, no one ever made any comment to you, nobody asked you any questions about where you came from?"

"Nothing. I was adopted completely. I was the little Parisian who had simply melted into the countryside. As people said then—and me too, because I spoke the local dialect, I can still speak it—I was a *drôlesse d'ici* [pronounced *ee-she*]. In Poitevin the word *drôlesse* is not pejorative at all!"[22]

"Had news from your father perhaps alerted you?"

"Of course. He hadn't spoken to me about the roundups in 1941, but he told me when Mother was arrested on July 16th, 1942, during the Vel' d'Hiv' roundup. My mother's arrest was the first that I heard about. It came as a terrible shock. I was learning at first hand about the persecution of Jews.

"It was the first time that they took women and children as well. And it was starting then that public opinion in Paris began to change, and the start of efforts to save the children. Some police inspectors assigned to Police Headquarters had snuck out and had warned people that a roundup was going to happen the following day. My mother didn't believe it. 'Why would they arrest women and children!' She was afraid for my father and for my brother, she insisted that they go and hide at the neighbors, in a street nearby. She stayed at home and she was arrested at dawn. All of my own fears stemmed from this.

"My father was worried about me from the moment he learned that I was known at the Town Hall. He had found out that children like me risked being arrested as well. He had asked the wife of a Belgian Jew, herself a gentile, to come and get me and hide me along with him in Paris somewhere. We must have just missed each other because I was arrested in the meantime. I wasn't always lucky, as you can see. A bit of bad luck also came my way."

"How did your being declared at Town Hall go down?"

"It was at the end of 1941 or early in '42, my brother came to work on a farm that had been found to take him in. Since he was 18 years old, he had an identification card that had had 'Jew' stamped on it, I don't know how, possibly during an identity check, the state police found out that he had a little sister somewhere nearby. If I received that set of stars, it was because they knew. It all came from that. I have no other explanation."

"So the sound of the car woke you. Did you get up right away? Did you hear voices?"

"I guess that Alice opened the door onto the courtyard. The policemen tell her that they have orders to arrest me. She objects: 'You are not going to take away this child, that isn't possible!' One of the policemen insists: 'We have orders, and if we don't find her, we'll take your husband!' Alice comes into my room. She says to me: 'The police are here, they have come to arrest you!' . . . For a split second I thought about escaping through a window onto the courtyard, that the neighbors would all take me in. But Alice added: 'They say that if they don't find you, they are taking Paul.' All that was left for me to do was to pack. I was supposed to take a change of clothing, and food for three days."

These were in fact the instructions given to the police by the regional authorities, except for the additional advice to be "discreet," whence the fact that this was happening in the middle of the night, and a Sunday at that! Added to which was the unwritten recommendation to proceed in teams of three men so that the arresting officers could observe each other and would be less tempted to disobey. Ida always liked to insist that they had to send three armed men to arrest her. Did they think it was necessary to be afraid of her, this fourteen-year-old girl, that they went to such lengths!

One will recall that Ida could have slipped out the back, and that the threat to arrest Alice's husband convinced her to give herself up . . . willingly. Doesn't what she modestly describes as a "normal" reflex in fact qualify as "heroic," coming as it does from a child of fourteen—and what a contrast to the pathetic zeal of the policemen, her first persecutors? This difference of opinion regarding the merits of what she did is among the rare points that the two authors of this book disagreed upon.

* * *

"What feeling did they give you, these two cops who obviously cared more for the Germans than for a girl from the country?"

Ida didn't hesitate for a moment to answer:

"At the time, nothing at all. Nothing but contempt!"

"And then? How about today?"

"I have always thought that they could have disobeyed orders and said something, that they couldn't find me, maybe, or that their car had broken down . . . but with three of them there, what could they do? For sure the whole thing could have been avoided right then without too much risk for the people who would have spared me!"

In fact, very few state employees disobeyed orders, and few of the ones who actually did refuse commands deemed unacceptable were punished for it by loss of life or imprisonment, or any other sanctions for that matter. We will learn later on what became of these overzealous backups of barbarism after the war. But we will never know what was going through their minds at the time when they were arresting Ida, since they were not asked about it then, nor were they inclined to reveal their thoughts on their own. Only one of them expressed being unhappy about it, as we shall see in just a moment, in the car during the drive to the police station in Melle.

Does Ida have any inkling of what is about to happen to her?

"I don't know. I have been thinking about deportation after all, since my mother had not been heard from since she was arrested a year and a half earlier. But we have no idea of the camps. It is only in Drancy that people will start me hoping that I will see my mother.[23] All that I knew was that I was being arrested although I had done nothing, solely because I was Jewish."

"What did you take with you?"

"An outfit that I had knit for myself entirely on my own, in raw wool, pleated, magnificent, and a handsome dark purple coat, with leather edging around the collar, that my father had made for me. I kept these until I reached the camp."

"You didn't cry?"

"I didn't cry. I am terrified, naturally, but I keep my fear to myself. No way I am going to give them the satisfaction of seeing me cry!"

"Any other preparations you had made?"

Ida's face lights up like a teenager who is about to tell a secret:

"I cut up the letters I had been keeping from a friend in the village and flushed them down the toilet, from a boy named Raymond whom I was in love with. Thinking about Alice, whose strictness I knew well, these tender yet really quite innocent letters between fourteen-year-olds seemed to me to be more compromising than the letters from my father, which as it happened I had been destroying all along!"

The memory of these letters from her father clearly moves her:

"My father signed his letters 'Rampou,' which is kind of like Thingamabob in Yiddish folklore."

Another detail pops out:

"I very quickly tore open the shoulder pads of my coat where my mother had hidden two twenty-dollar gold pieces, 'just in case.' Think about that a bit: in those days Jews felt so threatened that they had the reflex to convert their savings into the most easily transported form possible! Before leaving I gave the pieces to Alice, without the policemen seeing. Before that, while I was packing my bag, the mayor's assistant, Monsieur Bouffard, and Alice's brother, Charles Goimier, whom she had tipped off, showed up to try and argue against my being taken away with the officer in charge, without success. . . . As for the packet of provisions—probably things which would keep, pork rinds, jam, honey—I didn't open it until Birkenau, where it was taken away from me. I had kept it, untouched, thinking that I would give it to my mother, since from Drancy on people kept telling me that I was going to join her. . . .

"Did Alice cry when the car pulled away?"

"A lot. She was very emotional."

"And you?"

"I already said: *I didn't cry.* I don't recall shedding a single tear. I can't recall taking out my handkerchief. I didn't want to make Alice feel any worse. And I didn't want to give the police the satisfaction. At moments like that, one feels an inner strength. A question of dignity. No, and no again, I didn't cry!"

"In the car, did you ask the policemen where they were taking you?"

"I didn't say a word. After the war, Alice told me that she asked them. I didn't hear them, but according to Alice one of them answered: 'We don't know. What is for sure is that *you won't be seeing her again.*' It was very cruel of them to say that, don't you think?"

"How did they know that there was no chance you'd come back?"

"I have no idea. In Niort they undoubtedly knew more. But in Melle . . .

There is an official report of the arrest, drawn up by the Melle brigade. In it they state that Ida was informed of "the German orders pursuant to which" she had been arrested, that she had been searched and was found to be carrying "no weapon on her person." These details are all recorded in the language of the administration, clearly intended to make the operation official, and all three of the policemen affixed their names to it.

In the black Traction, which pulls out of the road where the Marché farm was situated and heads toward Melle, Ida is positive that she didn't say a single word, nor did the policemen. Except for the one next to whom and under whose watch she was placed, in the rear of the vehicle. She can still see the scene play out, pathetic and ridiculous:

"He took off his *képi*,[24] he wiped his brow with a large handkerchief—with checks, I haven't forgotten the handkerchief—and he sighed: 'What a nasty job!'"

This was the only comment during the trip to headquarters. Upon arrival, at after two in the morning, she is presented to captain T., who is waiting in full uniform, standing behind his desk, in front of the portrait of Pétain.[25] They didn't put handcuffs on the child, but one of the cops is holding her by the arm. With this many people looking after her, there is no question of her trying to escape. The certificate of French nationality that Alice had supplied didn't help at all. The officer was interested in one thing, and one thing alone: to know the address of Ida's dad. Not a word about her mother, who had been arrested in 1942. He questions her, hard but without brutality.

"I reply that I don't know where my father is (in fact I always wrote to him at the address where he used to live, near Paris, at the home of a man named Lagneau). The captain didn't believe me. He tried to frighten me."

Failing to get this information out of her, they drove Ida to Niort, to a huge hangar where there were cots set up everywhere. She learned afterwards that there would be 58 Jews gathered there, men, women, and children, arrested during the night across the region. The January 30th roundup would go down as one of the biggest ever in the department.

"There was no one that you recognized at this depot?"

"No one. I was the only hidden Jew in the village. One finds out about these things. I remember one couple, they seemed to me to be older people at the time, who took an interest in me, and looked out for me. By deduction, a bit later on, I figured out that they were named Friedmann. No one said anything about where we were headed, which was a mystery to all of us."

The next morning Alice showed up! The officers who were guarding the entrance let her pass.

"She was crying so hard! She says how she went to see the priest in Sompt at first light and that he had given her a fake certificate of baptism. The son-in-law of the mayor's assistant had driven her to Niort, using the last gas that he had. You have to try and imagine the courage that this took: she who had never said a word to a German soldier, here she was at the *Kommandantur*.[26] She is met by the officer in charge. She shows the certificate, she swears that her lodger has been arrested by mistake.

The conversation between the officer of the Reich and the *poitevine* peasant has a tragic twist to it:

The officer: "Who arrested her?"

Alice: "The French police."

The officer: "In that case, you understand, madame, I cannot intervene!"

In thus placing the blame on the French for all of the arrests that Vichy had taken credit for since the Oberg-Bousquet agreements,[27] for the occupying power to thus wash its hands of an infamy that it had in fact demanded, and which it obviously had the authority to stop, these Germans were indeed taking perverse pleasure in mocking the entire defeated French nation in the person of this defenseless farm woman.

"Alice came back to the depot. 'He just made fun of me!' she kept saying, through her tears.

"The following night they came to get me, along with three other children. They led us on foot to a hospital, with just one policeman. I thought again about running away, for one last time during the arrest, but I was afraid, I didn't know anyone, as I had back in Lié. The nuns were very kind to us. I thought that we were going to stay there. . . . But the next day they brought us back to the depot, saying that one of the women who was there had succeeded in helping two of her children to escape. I didn't believe it was a matter of reprisals, and I remember thinking: 'In any case they would have caught us; if this woman managed to get two of her kids to escape, bravo! She did the right thing!'"

The mother was deported to Auschwitz in the same train as Ida. She never came back. The children survived. It is worth noting, even if the concerned individual only sees a "natural" reflex in the mother's doing what she did, whatever the consequences might have been for the group and for herself. Ida was learning, at the age of fourteen, nothing less that the spirit of resistance!

That evening two extra passenger cars were hooked up to the Niort-Paris train that traveled via Poitiers. It was more than what was required, even with twenty policemen on board, as the roundup of the Jews from the Deux-Sèvres had "only produced" fifty-eight people.

Exhausted by the first nights of detention and travel, Ida no longer remembers what means of transport was used to transfer them to Drancy. There was no rail link from the Austerlitz train station to the internment camp that was opened in 1941 in the northern suburbs of Paris. It is likely that the transfer was done by bus. Some Parisians do recall buses of the TRCP—as the RATP was called in those days[28]—buses with the long square engine compartment and the rear platform that scraped the pavement, parked alongside the train station, full of passengers who were apparently coerced and under heavy guard. Under the pseudonym Forez, François Mauriac[29] recalled such a vision, accompanied by children shouting. He told his son Claude about it, and the son confirmed it. Such are the rebuttals to those Parisians who claimed, and still claim, that they "knew" nothing of this.

Drancy—Pitchipoï

Ida does not remember much about the week she spent in Drancy.

"What struck me was the height of the apartment buildings. I wasn't used to that. In the countryside I had grown used to low, isolated farmhouses. It seemed to me to be huge and . . . intense. People running every which way, as if they were very busy doing something, one knew not what, and in a hurry, while at the same time nothing was happening, except for the formation of convoys, which usually took place on Thursdays. The men were all ordered to stand on one side, the women and children on the other. The Friedmanns continued to look out for me."

"Still no Germans in sight?"

"None, although everyone said that they were in charge of Drancy. Nothing but French police."

"What did the detainees do to occupy themselves?"

"In the mornings the women and children had peeling duties. We peeled rutabagas and turnips. . . . I can remember having problems with my identification papers. In principle, one didn't get an ID card until one reached sixteen years of age, but I was asked for one, doubtless because with my hair combed up high in front I looked older—which would prove to be extremely lucky for me later on. I was informed that my food ration card was not enough."

"What were people talking about? Did anyone suspect what was going to happen?"

"We knew that we were going to be deported in the coming days."

"Was this the first time you heard the word *deported* mentioned?"

"Yes and no. I had heard it with regard to my mother, in 1942. But about me, this was the first time."

"What did you think it meant?"

"We thought that we were going to work 'in camps in the East,' the famous 'Pitchipoï,' which means something kind of like 'the Boonies.' The name 'Auschwitz' was never spoken. I wasn't worried so much, really, because in the office we are assured that those of us who have parents that have already been deported will be reunited with them. I believed it. I clung to it. I was literally on a cloud, I was so convinced that I was going to find my mother that, in spite of the clear soup and the daily crust of bread in Drancy, I didn't touch the provisions that Alice had given me on the night of my arrest. Still convinced that I was going to find my mother soon, I kept the package unopened during the trip to Auschwitz! That crazy hope colors all my memories of Drancy. Except for that it is a black hole, until the moment we boarded the train.

"Since I must have arrived on the day following a departure, I didn't witness the formation of a 'transport' other than my own.

"It took place on February 10, 1944. Early in the morning, the thousand five hundred detainees designated for convoy number 68 were gathered together, counted, and pushed by the policemen into the buses of the TCRP. We were driven to the Bobigny[30] train station where we were turned over to Germans who were waiting for us on the platform, and who pushed us roughly into cattle cars. In the opening of each car there was a board in place because of the difference in height between the cars and the platform."

How can one explain the Germans' combination of mistreatment and hurriedness on the one hand and of preparedness on the other, almost as if they knew they were up to no good? Ida is certain:

"They were afraid of attracting the public's attention!"

Based on the work of Serge Klarsfeld,[31] the convoy consists of 674 men, 814 women and 218 persons under 18 years of age. They come from the roundups of February 3rd, 1944 (425) and of the 4th (469), as well as from the big roundup in the prefectural region of Poitiers that began on January 28th.

On the ride from Drancy to the station in Bobigny, Ida recalls having thrown a message out addressed to Alice. The message was delivered. It said that she had left for "an unknown destination." Apart from that, what she remembers is the old buses they were packed into, so loaded down that the back platforms scraped the pavement. (These are the same vehicles that will serve to transport the returning troops from the gare de l'Est to the Hotel Lutétia in May of 1945. Bertrand remembers this—he was a boy scout who had volunteered to help out! As for Ida, she would not need them when she was repatriated, as she was flown back to France and was delivered directly to the Hôpital Broussais.[32])

How many people *per* bus? Fifty, sixty, seventy? Ida does not know. It seems that each vehicle corresponded to a train car that was ready to depart. Ida recalls seeing on the station platform French uniforms, *gardes mobiles,*[33] and ordinary police (the same police force that would be decorated upon Liberation!). But this time it is armed Germans who are taking delivery, and oversee boarding the train. This latter consists of at least twenty cars designed for horses, to hold the fifteen hundred people to be deported.

Outside, the history of the world war is tipping. On the 10th of January, 1944, Victor Basch and his wife are assassinated.[34] The siege of Leningrad was broken on the 14th of January. The Representative Council of Israelites of France (the CRIF) was founded on January 5th.[35] The French Forces of the Interior (the FFI) will be in February.[36] On the 6th of February, Klaus Barbie has the children of Izieu arrested.[37] The *maquis* on the Glières plateau is wiped out in March, but the ultimate defeat of the Reich was only a matter of months away.[38] The Allies are working their way up the Italian boot. They will come ashore in Normandy in four months.

The German soldiers who "take delivery" of convoy number 68 can therefore not be unaware that their Hitlerian dream of a thousand years of military supremacy and the eradication of "inferior races" is about to vanish. And yet, the "final solution" put in place in Wannsee,[39] continues to be carried out, in crisp uniforms, riding crop at the ready, and dogs at heel.

Among the detainees, whom the SS[40] shove into the train cars like so many animals, allow us to linger a moment over the profile of Ida, among the hundreds of others. She is wearing the skirt, the sweater, and coat that she wore when she left the farm in Lié. On her feet, shoes typical of that time of shortages, with hinged wooden soles. She is wearing over her shoulder a little handbag in golden brown leather that her father gave her for her fourteenth birthday, the work of a leather-craftsman cousin of his with whom he is in hiding. In the bag, which she finds "ravishing," there only remain such useless treasures as children carry. The 360 francs that Alice had slipped her—an enormous amount for the farm woman—were confiscated when Ida arrived at Drancy in exchange for a dubious receipt.

Above her forehead, Ida sports the fashionable wave of hair that her mother did for her, which will luckily cause her to be placed among the adults able to work. Her cheeks still have, for a little while yet, the roundness that years of life in the country have given her. Thinking back on it, she thinks that she appeared a little bit older than her age, and strong, ready for the very worst, which was speeding towards her . . .

Is it really so certain? When her daughter Sophie reached the age she was at when she left Bobigny, Ida was beside herself with anxiety over how vulnerable the girl seemed. "I was fortunate, she thought, to be tougher than Sophie at age fourteen."

How can one not have some of the same fear for Ida that she had for her daughter, when one thinks about the barking of the SS men, the screeching of iron and the clanging of bolts, as the heavy door slams shut on the face of the child!

PART II

From a Human to an Item

"It Couldn't Be Any Worse!"

The last glimpse of the civilized world vanished with the little antiquated railroad station of Bobigny (a memorial site, if there ever was one, that people have not given up saving from the wrecker's ball).[1] Hell begins here. It begins with the final closure of the boxcar, whose single skylight is a slender barred rectangle opening onto a winter sky.

It has often been said: no place to lie down on the bare plank floor, scarcely room to sit on a few sticks of straw. In the middle of the space, a bucket of water, soon empty, and a bucket to use as a toilet, soon full. Grinding iron wheels, the gasping of the steam locomotive, spurts of soot, complaints, whimpers. For sustenance, a chunk of bread *per* person. A single stop in open country, the second day, snow on the embankments, probably in Germany already, guards standing alongside the track, raincoats covering the tops of their boots, weapons at the hip. . . . But still not a word about the destination, nor about how long the nightmare would last.

The true nature of the torture promised to the deportees is clearly revealed in the systematic lack of respect, a ferocity that was as implacable as it was unseen. Whatever the ultimate intention might be, still hidden as it was, it becomes clear that they are hearing themselves referred to not as humans but simply as cargo, reduced to a mere quantity. In the camp they will be referred to as "*stück*" instead of as people, which is to say as pieces, as items, and soon as numbers without names. "We need one thousand a week," Vichy told its prefectural leaders. If foreign

Jews no longer furnished enough, the prefects had only to "make up" the number with "some" French Jews: no sooner said than done. As the use of boxcars reaffirmed, it was only so much stuff that was being transported.

The first real horror? Ida doesn't hesitate:

"The stench! The first humiliation that we had to endure was to go to the toilet in front of everyone. So we got 'organized.'"

Please note the word "organized"; it will come to mean coping, barter, deal-making, but always in a community-oriented way, free of any contemporary "every man for himself" connotation, a building block of survival solidarity.

"Two adults would each hold a coat, one on each side, to protect us as best they could against loss of dignity. The bucket was overflowing in no time. The contents spilled on the straw. Pretty soon the air was rank and unbreathable."

"Were there any other kids your age?"

"I think so. The same ones from the hangar/depot in Niort. I wasn't next to them. I was in a corner with the Friedmann couple and two young girls from Brittany. There was a child younger than me in a family with three kids. But no actual infants."

"No way that you could actually sleep?"

"We barely had room to sit down. We could lean our head on our neighbor's shoulder, with the solidarity of stable animals! One drifted off."

"Did you talk?"

"Very little."

"About what?"

"About what it would be like where we were going. From the very beginning Mrs. Friedmann said to me: 'When we get there I'll take care of you, you'll see.' Me, I was still thinking I would find my mother. I don't remember being hungry. I probably finished my piece of bread right away. But I still had Alice's provisions with me. There was no way I was going to break into them. I was keeping them for my mother. I thought that after a year and a half in the camp that she would be really happy to receive some nice things. In fact I didn't even tell anyone that

I had any food. It was my secret treasure. . . . There were no really old people, no one who was very sick. We didn't wash, of course. We just sat there like so much livestock."

"Did the guards speak?"

"When we stopped, they began shouting like they always do, they don't know how to speak in any other way. Those of us who could jump down from the height of the car went and relieved ourselves on the side of the track, car by car. And we got under way again."

Every turn of the wheels brought them closer to something that they staunchly refused to imagine. Still the myth about Pitchipoï. As we say today, they "managed" their expectations. Only one thing seemed certain, and about this they all agreed: "It couldn't go on forever." And at the end of the trip, even if no one imagined the reality of the camp or believed that death would follow more or less quickly, the general belief was that "it couldn't be worse than this." Compared to the harshness of the present circumstances this certainty about the future could be construed as "hope." When they arrived in Auschwitz everybody let out a shout of relief: "Finally, we are there!"

"There were those who cried out of despair. But there was simply no question of resisting, or of trying to run away. We didn't even know what regions we were crossing. We were groggy with sleepiness, following three days and three nights and nearly two thousand kilometers.[2] Nobody went crazy from it, in my car, but I know that people did. There were no real fights, as also happened elsewhere. No escape attempts either. In cars where the men tried to pry up the floorboards, women stopped them out of fear of reprisals. I can imagine convoys in the summer, like that of my mother, in July 1942, must have suffered more than those in winter, on account of heat and thirst. There were other girls, but I remember in particular the two from Brittany."

Out of 1,500 people in convoy number 68—one of the largest ever—of the 210 men and of the 61 women selected on arrival, only 42 returned, including 24 women.

"On Another Planet!"

Most everyone is familiar with the macabre irony of the motto inscribed in wrought iron over the entrance at Auschwitz: *Arbeit macht frei*, "Work will make you free." It would have been more honest to declare: "Work is life," or even: "Inability to work is death!" Ida will prove this to be true within hours of arrival:

"My first bit of luck was just that, that I went and stood, without being aware of it, on the side of the women who were old enough and strong enough to work. This instinctive decision would mean the difference between immediate extermination and slow death from exhaustion.

"It was February 13th, 1944. A Sunday morning, as usual: the trains left Drancy on Thursdays and arrived on Sunday. When the train stopped, with a particularly brutal jolt that I still remember, it was a great relief. We had 'reached the absolute bottom'; or at least we thought so. 'Finally!' we sighed. I had the added thought: 'This is it, I am going to find mother!' We suspected that we were about to arrive, we had seen the names of stations in German along the way, without knowing that we were in Poland already.

"First sensation: an infernal hubbub, a combination of the slamming open of train car doors, orders yelled out—*Schnell! Raus!*[3]—the barking of dogs, the screams from families being broken up. When an arrival occurred at night, the spotlights completed the nightmare atmosphere. I believe that it was on purpose, it was part of a script that was being played out. Later on, the train would go all the way to the entrance of

Birkenau,[4] but at this time it stopped in open country about two and a half kilometers from the gate of the camp. We walked the rest of the way. There was a lot of snow on the ground.

"Along the way, men in striped pajamas translated the shouts of the SS men. They were in charge of 'receiving' us. Some of the deportees spoke with these men, I did not. Thanks to my knowledge of Yiddish, I understood the orders; this will often be useful to me in the camp, I will translate for comrades, I will avoid getting beaten for not obeying orders quickly enough.

"Unlike in Bobigny, there are no planks to help get down out of the trains. At Auschwitz the floor of the car was over three and a half feet above the ground. We had to jump, although the snow helped soften the impact. Old people had trouble. The men were immediately separated from the women and children. I happened to be with the two girls from Brittany whom I had met in the train car.

"It was then that an incident occurred which probably sealed my destiny, but the consequences of which tortured me for a long time to come. In the crush of people on the platform, we were ordered to move toward the head of the train to take part in a roll call. I heard Mrs. Friedmann, the woman who had helped me in the train car: 'Ida, wait for me!' It was in order to continue looking after me, not because she needed help, but I had already set off with the girls for the rail-head where we were told to gather, and I don't know why, but I didn't wait for this woman. That was just how it was, I wanted to stay with the girls, I didn't want to risk losing sight of them by turning back. It still makes me sick every time I think about it. I felt guilty for a long time. I was far from imagining what was going to happen to people who remained behind, like her, it was unthinkable, but there you have it, my instinct led me to not respond to her call. I never saw my 'protector' again: she was among the ones who were gassed on arrival. . . .

"I never saw the girls from Brittany again in the camp, either. What I do know is that we started out in triage together. Because we ran, we arrived first at the meeting point, and we had to deal with a single SS man and not with a bunch of them, as I learned later was usually the case.

"There were rows of gray trucks parked alongside the train. We learned after the war that one of the trucks, which was marked with a Red Cross to reassure us, was actually carrying Zyklon B for use in the gas chambers.

"The SS man, who was carrying a riding crop, ordered in very bad French that anyone who could not walk should get into the trucks while the rest of us were told to wait on the platform. Without further ado, I said to myself 'I am not tired,' and I immediately joined the women who were going to continue on foot. The SS did not ask me anything about my age, nor did he guess it. I looked more like sixteen, with my healthy country-girl cheeks and the famous high wave of hair that my mother had done for me instead of my ringlets at spring break in April of 1942! So my mother gave me life twice, once at birth, and a second time by making me look older. Fortunately, because at age fourteen I was supposed to go with the group of people who were gassed on arrival!

"So I was among the sixty-one women selected to enter the camp. Twenty-four of us would survive. This is partly due to the fact that this was in 1944. We would only spend two winters in Auschwitz. One more winter and we wouldn't have made it. The number of survivors from 1942 is miniscule. The 754 women who got into the trucks were gassed right away along with the children. We naively thought that the trucks were there to help the infirm, out of . . . humanity, of some kind!

"The camp of Birkenau, to which we were directed, was a part of a complex called Auschwitz, the center of which was three kilometers away. Birkenau was the largest of forty 'sub-camps.' It was designed to hold one hundred thousand prisoners, and it was where the gas chambers and crematoria were. Most of the photographs of Auschwitz show, in reality, the entrance to Birkenau, with its central guard tower. The railroad track was eventually extended to pass under this archway so that the convoys could roll into the camp and stop right next to the crematoria. At the time of my arrival the trains still stopped far in front of the camp.

"Before directing us to make our way on foot to Birkenau the soldiers insisted that we leave our belongings, in a heap, in the snow, without any tags identifying them—all simply lost. I have to throw away the little leather purse where I was keeping pictures of my parents, and the package of food that I was still planning on giving to my mother. It breaks my heart when it happens. I have nothing left from my former life! . . . As we walk in we see no one because the prisoners have all gone to work. We see nothing but filthy run-down buildings and, through the windows, a few pale women wearing scarves on their head, who stare at us with a dull, far-off look. This time we have really landed on another planet!

"At the entrance we are told to go into a large room called the 'Secretariat.' Some Polish women prisoners wearing civilian clothing who didn't look too badly treated, physically, make us fill out identification slips. Without thinking, I write down my true age. One of the employees appears to hesitate over what I have written. It is my age that surprises her, but in my obsession with finding my mother, I imagine that this woman has noticed my name, and that she knows my mother. Like all of the other Jewish girls, I am required to put Sarah in front of my name. From here on I will be known as Sarah-Ida. The men all have to call themselves Israel-something.

"From there we are all herded into a large hall called 'Disinfection,' the sauna, with two exits. We are flabbergasted. We don't ask questions, but we fear the worst. There are three SS and a man in civilian clothing, possibly a doctor. We are ordered to get completely undressed. We were all struck motionless. None of us dared to get undressed. It seemed unthinkable to us to get undressed in front of these soldiers. To require that of us seemed like an outrage. We tried to keep our underwear on. But right away they shouted louder: '*Nackt!*'[5] They want us completely naked.

"Women wearing armbands designating them as '*Kapo*' appear and begin to beat us with rubber truncheons. It was the first time that we had seen these people. The *Kapos* were common criminals who were recognizable by the black triangle that preceded the identification number on their clothing. The Germans had recruited them in their civil prisons for service as auxiliaries to keep order in the camps. In exchange these people received certain advantages: individual rooms, clothing, food, etc. They had complete authority over us, including the right to beat us.

"Other female prisoners who don't speak French arrive to take away our clothing, which was left everywhere on the floor. We understand that we won't see any of it again. They remove any jewelry that hadn't been taken from us at Drancy. I lost my earrings. I didn't have a watch or a chain. Married women had to give up their wedding bands. I notice that all of this loot is being collected in my little leather purse that I loved so. I will never know how this bag that I gave up at trackside on arrival managed to get to the Sauna so quickly. Some of our group later saw their clothes being worn by *Kapos*. As for me, I never got any of my things back.

"That was when yet other prisoners[6] appeared in groups equipped with hair clippers in hand and they cut off all of our hair, armpits and pubis included. It was terribly humiliating. You don't see yourself, of course, but you see the effect it has when you make out other women who are scarcely recognizable, disfigured. Since the fashion then was for long hair, there was a real carpet of hair on the floor, long locks, brown and chestnut. Some women are in tears. Personally, I did not shed a tear, I did not want to give them that satisfaction. But all the same I said to myself: If they are treating us like this now, what on earth lies in store?

"More prisoners come out, this time armed with pens and inkwells. We are all tattooed on the left forearm. The numbers all follow those of the prior convoy. They correspond to our date of arrival in the camp. My number is 75360. When we are sent to the shower, one of my numbers partly ran off. I worried about this, because I figured I would have to know it by heart, and I did not really know what a tattoo was then (in the country, in those days, they didn't tattoo the animals!). One of the women tapped my cheek and reassured me: 'Don't worry, she said, the rest of your number isn't about to come off.' In fact, the inscription is still there after almost sixty years now![7]

"What came next was supposed to relieve us from the cold and of our shame: we were thrown bundles of civilian clothing. But this consisted of a kind of dress with a little jacket that didn't keep you warm at all. The cloth was a kind of woven rayon called *fibrane*. The striped pajamas would come later. These were civilian clothes of dubious provenance that had been put through an industrial wash. They probably belonged to some long-gone prisoners. There was a big red cross painted on the back, just in case anyone tried to escape. Shoes are tossed to us without regard as to size. We exchange them among ourselves as best we can. I remember one woman whose clogs were so big that they fell off when she walked.

"Here we are then, disguised, reduced to a number on the forearm, without identity, without a past or a future, tossed into the hell of the concentration camp system in a single morning. That afternoon we were served a bowl of soup with some vaguely cabbage-like bits floating in it. It is as well a new level in our dehumanization, since with neither a spoon nor a personal bowl of any sort, we were forced to lap up our portion like animals. I chose not to touch it.

"That evening we find ourselves in the 'Quarantine' block.[8] This hygiene precaution is absurd. In their obsession with disinfection, the Germans ought to know that microbes are more prevalent in Auschwitz than in the countries that we come from. I realize that my two friends are not in the same block as I am. I don't know anyone around me anymore.

"But fortunately, from the first night, we are visited by some French prisoners, who snuck in after curfew. They take this risk every Sunday in order to get information from the newly arrived. Among them, there is Suzanne Birnbaum, a big woman with very bright eyes. She is about forty years old. She inquires about my age in her Parisian accent. She advises me to 'certainly not say a word about this to the *Kapos,* if they ask.' She adds: 'Because to youngsters like you they will often give an extra bowl of soup, and afterwards they disappear and we never see them again.' It was doubtless in connection with some 'experiments.'

"I decide that henceforth I will always say 'sixteen years,' if anyone asks. I owe this vital reflex to Suzanne. In fact, it is as if I was always sixteen, in my head. I grew older in one fell swoop. I will never have been fifteen! As for Suzanne, every time one ran into her, she lifted our spirits. She always found the right words to encourage us. She, too, would survive, which was unusual for a forty-year-old. As soon as she returned from the camps she wrote a book, which is out of print, but there is talk of publishing it again.[9]

"We asked our visitors about the fate of the women in our convoy who got into the trucks. Where did they go? To which barrack? Without hesitation and without trying to make it easier on us, they explained to us that these women were gassed on arrival, and burned in the crematory ovens whose smoke we could see from the windows of the 'Quarantine.' I can swear that at that moment not a single one of us believed it.

"It is beyond comprehension. There is no way we can confirm this by asking the heads of our blocks who speak Slovakian and who are not inclined to answer us. We think that our visitors have been in the camp for a long time, that they are making stuff up, that they have gone batty, embittered by what they have been through, and that the smoke comes from factories.

"It would take me four or five days to accept the obvious. I who had lived in the countryside, I could tell the difference between smells, that of burning fallen leaves, of wood, of roast pig. The truth would come to me during a roll call, one day when the wind carried the smoke in the direction of our barrack. I recognized the smell of burning flesh, and I said so to one of my comrades: this time there is no doubt about it, this is what we had been told. The most convincing proof: birds had deserted Auschwitz! Having arrived alone, and not having seen any of my own family head off toward the trucks, I had less difficulty accepting the unacceptable.

"It wasn't the same for my friend Claudine Chikman. She had been arrested in Nice together with her parents and her grandfather. She didn't want to believe that they had been gassed on arrival. After the war she explained to me that she had literally 'needed to doubt' in order to survive. On the platform, she had wanted to go with her mother, who was going to be put to death. Twice the SS had ordered her to let go of her mother's arm, which she was still clutching. Her mother begged her to obey, for fear the SS would beat her right there in front of her, which she wouldn't have been able to bear.

"Claudine's survival depended on this slender circumstance! It is likely that the same thing would have happened if I had followed Mrs. Friedmann upon climbing out of the train. I felt very guilty until the moment I realized I couldn't have saved her, any more than Claudine could save her mother, and that I would simply have disappeared along with her."

Ida never lost sight of the fact that friendship was their only path to survival. She is still overcome by a kind of enthusiasm, of pride, of gratitude for the energy that it provided them:

"Groups begin to form right away. Right away in quarantine, I meet some girls from my own convoy, so they speak French. Our barrack contains several hundred Jewish detainees, all women, of many different nationalities. Despite orders given by the block leader, we can make the acquaintance of whomever we wish. For example, in order to find space in the '*koyas*'—the frames of cement and wood where we slept in fives and sixes on each of three levels. By sheer luck I was on the top level, where there was enough headroom to sit up, one can remain seated to eat the chunk of bread handed out just before curfew, while below they are obliged to lie down."

"The day after our arrival in the quarantine section, we each receive a piece of cloth on which is printed our identification number, preceded by the star of David. We are supposed to sew it on the left side of our jacket at chest level. It is our ID card. It shows that we are Jewish, and the number indicates when we arrived.

"From this moment on, we will be referred to by this number alone, which we must know by heart in German or else we might be beaten. For French girls who didn't know Yiddish, this could be a challenge. I help them. My own number comes back to me automatically: *funf und siebzig tausend dreihundert sechzig*. Sometimes we also had to know it in Polish.

"We knew that there was typhoid fever in the camp. In quarantine, two girls who were identified with it were evacuated to the infirmary. They had to be dragged out. They refused to leave for the *Revier*.[10] We knew that it was the gateway to death. The girls struggled. They cried. Their sobbing was painful to all of us. We all watched this drama, unable to do a thing about it. . . . The soup they served us caused diarrhea. I avoided this mostly because I ate as little as possible, although my comrades made me eat 'if I wanted to see France again.' The soup? Clear water, warm, with bits of rutabagas, of cabbage. There were more consistent vegetables, like potatoes, but the *Kapos* kept these for themselves by not stirring the bottom of the pots. The girls who worked in the kitchen could have a little extra, but not us.

"Our first experience of the latrines was a moment of utter shock. They were located in a large barrack fairly far from ours. The utter filth and stench that hangs over the building are unimaginable. It houses a long bench made of concrete with dozens of holes along its two sides. Each seat is more or less splattered with fecal matter (most of the prisoners already suffered from dysentery). We have no means of cleaning the hole where we were obliged to sit, nor paper to wipe ourselves with. We are admitted together in groups of fifty. If one of us wants to stay a little longer, the *Kapo* drives her out with a stick. Another group is waiting to enter.

"The briefest instant of intimacy is forbidden. Not a single one of us was able to get used to this monstrous promiscuity. Some deportees have said that it was an opportunity to exchange news from inside the camp and from outside, but I do not remember that being the case with us. Nothing but revulsion that was more difficult to bear each time we went.

"Except for roll calls, we remain in our barrack. This was when we talked, especially among the teenagers from France. Each one tells her own story, her arrest. Hélène Ekajzer, for example, who had survived in Paris with a younger brother following the arrest of their mother in 1942 by reselling milk cut with water.

"We believe that the war will end and that our fate will depend on this. News of the landing in Normandy will bring us hope, but we did think that the Allies took forever to cross Europe. From June 1944 until May of 1945 was an awfully long time!

"After quarantine was over, whenever I run into French girls with numbers that are lower than mine, I tell them that I am looking for my mother, who must have arrived in July of 1942, and I ask them if there is any chance of talking to women who were in her convoy. Every time I get the same response, their arms thrown upwards: they don't know. It is only after several weeks that I give up hope of finding my mother."

In fact, everybody is living in the moment. When waking, before daybreak, they say to themselves: "I can't wait for evening to come!" And when they go to bed they think: "I made it through another day!"

One can hardly speak of there being a single big event during quarantine. Yet there was one. Ida recalls a first health crisis, which takes on an importance all its own when seen in retrospect.

In the very first days, she gets a sore throat, because of the drafts in the barrack. When she was four she had croup, a kind of diphtheria that often leaves one with a weakened throat. She feels a fever coming on. She is no tenderfoot and she wants to take effective action. She located a barrack "leader," a veteran of the Polish ghettos, who seemed to her to be nicer than the others. The barrack leaders were deportees who were in charge of maintenance of the block, and there were five or six of them in each barrack. They didn't work outside at all. They helped the head of the barrack to distribute rations. It was a relatively cushy job.

Ida asked one of these leaders in Yiddish to find her some very hot water and some salt. She went outside and gargled, as her mother, who favored traditional remedies, had taught her to do. She almost scalded herself she did it so hard, but she really wanted her improvised treatment to work. It was a matter of life and death.

As at the boarding of the train in Bobigny, one wishes one could zoom out and take in the entire scene: a child of fourteen treating herself as her mother had taught her, taking her destiny into her own hands, alone in the night of a barrack in Upper Silesia.[11]

Her effort was rewarded with success: the sore throat was immediately checked!

The Kapos*: "Here, You Enter Via the Door, and You Leave Via the Chimney!"*

People who have never experienced anything like this wonder if the prisoners still have the strength to think about what is happening to them, about the inhumanity of the guards. Do some of them have the reflex to ask or implore "Heaven"? Ida never received any Jewish religious education. The idea never occurred to her to turn toward the God of her ancestors. At this thought a smile crosses her face, one of irony free of any illusions.

"Given the way God forgot about us! It did occur to me that perhaps Alice prays to her God of the Christians on my behalf. Or perhaps the Virgin Mary, for whom she had a particular devotion. In some way I feel that I am under her protection. . . . As far as our thinking is concerned, it is limited to vital necessities. The big question is simply to hold on, to preserve one's dignity by whatever means. When we get back from work, our first thought is to wash, and to recover.

"We are barely aware of the passing of the seasons. In Poland, winter is endless, and spring is very short. It basically consists of the thaw, at the end of April. The thaw is terrible! Mud everywhere! There are so many of us walking on the bare ground. The earth turns into slush.

"The evening roll call is the longest, because it doesn't impinge on the work day. The guards make the operation last, as if they enjoyed it. We are exhausted. As far as 'roll call' is concerned, they don't check our names or our identification numbers. In fact all they want to do is count us. We have to add up to the number they are looking for. It is forbidden to speak, to move, to turn around, to stamp our feet on the ground to keep warm. If anyone among us feels unwell, it is forbidden to help them stand. We are not allowed to leave our places. It is out of the question to let them remain inside. The big fear is to be noticed, to be sent to the *Revier.*

"In quarantine, we remained in the barrack all day and only came out for roll calls. But when someone went missing from a work detail, they would replace her with one of us."

A Day in Quarantine

"In quarantine we all sleep in these bunks made out of cement—in Polish they are called *koyas*—which are different from the bunk beds that the men are in. Every *koya* consists of three levels, occupied by five or six deportees. The mattresses, very thin, are filled with sawdust. The comrades on the lowest level are the coldest, because they are sleeping on the ground. We have two blankets per level. We place one of them under us, and the other one to cover ourselves with. In order to keep warm we sleep one right next to the other. The ones on the outside never have enough blanket. Right away we work out a rotation so that it is not always the same ones who are cold. Out of sheer luck they didn't force us into sleep groups. We grouped ourselves into groups of French girls. There is a wood stove at each end of the barrack, but it is hardly any warmer inside than out of doors.

"The leader of the block and the secretary each occupy a small separate room, one facing the other, at the entrance to the barrack. Sometimes, when a door was left partly open we could see the interior of these rooms, nicely made up, comfortable. The sight of these rooms makes the conditions we live in even more difficult to bear.

"The heads of the barrack use the woodstove to make a kind of grub out of their special rations. We watch them cook some kind of dumplings. When they fry onions the smell drives us crazy with longing, it was real torture. At the start we are not really tired enough to fall asleep just like that. We are totally stressed out by what we are discovering every day, and by the complete lack of hygiene. We can barely exchange, in whispers, impressions on the harshness of the camp. We know that we are going to work. Hunger begins to get to us. Immediately the block leaders shout 'Silence!' in Polish.

"Towards four in the morning the *Kapo* shouts 'On your feet!' She grabs some of us, in turns, to go and fetch the kettle of 'Juice,' a kind of unsweetened barley broth. Here I really feel my age works against me: I can barely lift the container off of the floor. Each individual reacts according to her own personality. The famous Helene, who will later live through the adventure of the 'potatoes,' shows incredible nerve. She was already taking care of a younger brother in Paris, following the arrest of their parents. She is sixteen years old. I am the youngest in our group. I have a good attitude, no doubt because of my young age. Young people have a stronger will to survive than older people."

Roll Call

"Right after juice, which is only of interest because it is hot (we keep a little aside to kind of mop our faces with), it's time for roll call. We have to go outside. In February, in Upper Silesia, the temperature regularly falls to between 5 and 10 degrees Fahrenheit. We have to stand in rows of five, at attention. No moving. Wind and snow whip our faces. No handkerchiefs. The soldiers from the SS charged with verifying the count come by, move on, then come back again.

"We also have to drag out the bodies of any women who died in the night, in order for the count to be exact. (Since our group had arrived recently, we experienced no such losses during quarantine.) Very quickly we are frozen to the bone. When the guards aren't watching, we rub the back of the comrade in front of us, after which it's the turn of the comrades behind to warm us. Everyone must remain in place until the end of roll call, which is one of the worst moments of the entire day. It is even forbidden to stamp your feet. Our legs grow numb.

"In the very first roll calls we become aware that we have become mere items, units, pieces. These are the words our guards used when talking about us, on purpose, to make us aware of our insignificance. The roll call is not over until the *Aufseherin*[12] has pronounced the magic word: *stimmt*—the count stands! During quarantine we can now go back inside. Later on, we will head off to work, for a twelve-hour workday.

"Noon is time for soup, which first has to be hauled from the kitchen. Every day I dreaded being assigned to carry the enormous barrels! After the evening roll call we are given a piece of bread, usually two slices of black bread, with a small blob of margarine, or a slice of sausage, or a spoonful of very runny marmalade. Later on we will earn the right to an additional piece of bread in the evening. Out of the question to drink at night, the water is not drinkable. The snow outside is too dirty to quench our thirst. By then it is curfew time, and it's forbidden to go outside.

"News from outside the camp is very rare. We will learn about the Allied landings from the women from convoys that arrived after June 6th. We will learn about the liberation of Paris in the same way. But the news from the camp takes precedence over everything. For example there is the drama surrounding Isabelle, a twenty-year-old from the countryside who revealed to us one day that she was pregnant without her family's knowing it at the time she was arrested. Since her pregnancy (of three months) couldn't really be noticed when she arrived in the camp, she was not sent for immediate extermination as was the rule with women in advanced pregnancy. We were worried for her. The block leader was the first to notice and immediately had her sent to another barrack.

"One Sunday—we had one Sunday in seven off—Isabelle comes to see us with the baby in her arms. The infant, a boy, is about a month old. He isn't all that skinny. She had found clothing and food for him. She is radiant with joy. . . . Shortly after that she comes back to see us and she is utterly miserable. Some comrades learned from her how they killed her baby right in front of her; but they hid this news from me, doubtless in order to spare the youngest one, which I was. We never saw Isabelle again. I would search very hard for her when the war was over because I liked her a lot. She must have died before the evacuation."

The Kommandos

"After quarantine, that is, three weeks later, we change barracks. The deportees are sent to different *Kommandos.*[13] The assignment of these jobs was random, or just based on appearance. A *Kapo* shows up, she picks some workers, and off they go. At first, we wanted to be picked, we figured that working would help time pass more quickly. But the first ones to be selected explained to us that it was difficult work, and could even involve hardship. In any case, we had no choice in the matter. You had better be healthy. But there is no hygiene at all, and despite the monthly disinfections, we are all infested with lice. There is no access to wash basins. There are too many of us. Moreover there are some women, Ukrainians in particular, who are monopolizing the faucets. Dysentery makes its appearance starting in quarantine.

"We tell ourselves that if we get pimples, *Krätze,* or mange, which the Germans dread, we risk the very worst. We learn that in addition to the initial selection, there are occasional other selections when we have to come naked in front of doctors who record the numbers of the weakest ones, or ones with pimples. They will be sent to 'Block 25,' from which they will be sent to the gas chamber two days later. Their whimpering and cries could be heard in the neighboring barracks.

"So it was vital to get to a source of water, by whatever means possible. In a gesture of complete madness, Suzanne and Lea Schwartzmann, two sisters who had recently arrived from Rheims who were a little older than me, got the idea that we should go out after curfew in order to try and reach the wash basins. Once or twice a week we would sneak out in the darkness between the barracks, at the risk of being caught by the *kapos* or spotted from a watch tower, which meant being beaten . . . or shot. Alone, I would never have dared do it.

"We have no soap and no towels, but at last we can wash with cold running water, with all the faucets for us. It is a miracle that we were never caught. But at least we didn't have pimples!"

Except for the sore throat and her feet being completely frozen during the evacuations, Ida never caught any of the diseases that were prevalent in the camp. She believes that she got thinner less quickly than her friends. She explains it by what she calls her "good attitude," her young age, and the stock of good health that she had built up over several years of country living, free of the deprivations of city folk.

"We all shared our life stories. Myself, I talked mostly about my life before the war. One always finds people more unlucky than oneself. The sisters from Rheims, for example. They are a very numerous family. They arrived in Auschwitz eight days before me with ten brothers and sisters plus the parents. Only Suzanne was selected on arrival. Lea wanted to go with her mother. Her mother told her to go with her sister instead. The entire family was pushed toward the trucks, that is to say, toward immediate death. The two survivors figured that out pretty quickly. They didn't believe it at first, but then it became obvious. As soon as one starts to work one realizes what is going on. The *kapos* don't hide it from us. When they are counting us or beating us they say over and over again in German 'Here, you come in through the door and you go out via the chimney!' I understand, thanks to my Yiddish. Even the ones that don't speak German figure it out pretty fast!"

Among all of the stories of her comrades, Ida holds her friend Liliane Badour's in a place all its own.

"Liliane came from Biarritz.[14] She had been arrested with her two young brothers, who were seventeen and thirteen years of age. She feared the very worst for them. The three of them had lost their father and mother. Liliane had been taking care of her brothers forever. Her reflex of being a big sister led her to take care of me. In fact, I was possibly better prepared than she, who didn't understand a word of German. I translated the *kapos'* orders for her for better or for worse.

"Alas, our friendship was going to be brutally ended. One day, near the start of quarantine, a *kapo* showed up to take some detainees to a *kommando* that was short a few women. Just by chance, she grabbed Suzanne, one of the two girls from Rheims, separating her from her sister Lea. Both of them cried out at the same time: 'I want to stay with my sister!' Without a moment's hesitation, Liliane offers herself to take Suzanne's place so that the two sisters can remain together."

Unfortunately, Liliane will be assigned to the worst *kommando* of all. For several months during the harsh winter she will work laying railroad track to allow the convoys to roll into Birkenau right up to the crematoria. As they worked without gloves, the workers' hands stuck to the frozen iron rails, causing cuts that wouldn't heal. Later on, Ida ran into Liliane again, on the day shift at the Union Werke factory . . .

Before the end of quarantine, Ida recalls a transaction that shows how important the struggle to maintain one's dignity could be.

"In the evenings. I usually shared my meager ration with Suzanne and Lea. It is comforting to share, however little food there is. But we can no longer stand to lap up our soup like animals. We 'organize' ourselves to get our hands on some spoons. The exchange rate for a spoon in the camp's barter system is one ration of bread for one spoon. We are obliged to make do with two rations for three people for several days in a row until we each have a spoon. One cannot imagine how precious this object was to us, the only thing that we possessed. The dignity that a simple spoon accorded us was of such value that we were ready to pay for it with even greater deprivation."

Towards the Kommandos

Assignments to *kommandos* happened after three or four weeks in quarantine. There is the *kommando* for rocks and sorting frozen potatoes, which Ida will be a part of. There is also sorting shoes and the clothing confiscated from new arrivals (in the area is called "Canada"), as well as any food they had with them. Ida's precious package, that she never saw again, must have passed through there, and found a taker! While waiting for an assignment, they introduced themselves to each other and shared memories, each one trying to instill fresh courage in them all.

The first *kommando* is the one known as "rocks." If only it consisted of earth-moving that had any visible purpose, any end! The only comprehensible purpose of the work was to wear people out, to discourage, degrade, and humiliate. They carry stacks of enormous rocks from one side of the quarry to the other on pallets made of planks, and then carry them back again. It lasts for twelve hours a day, from six in the morning until six in the evening.

"I haven't remembered the exact dates. I know that we are still in winter, and that winter is lasting into May. But then I got sent to the commando [*sic*] of 'spuds.' This takes place in a hangar with clerestory windows all around. There are gigantic piles of potatoes, all frozen hard. Our job is to sort out the least rotten among them, supposedly for our soup, but the *Kapos* never stir it when serving us, the better to share the good part with the other guards. There is nothing on top but some floating cabbage leaves. This knowledge makes our drudgery even more aggravating."

The potato *Kommando* is the scene of a memorable funny incident.

"The awesome girl whom I mentioned earlier, Helene (she survived and died only a few years ago), decides to hide some potatoes in her clothing in the hope of cooking and eating them on the sly. I am afraid of reprisals. She insists. She puts the potatoes in her sleeves, her pockets, everywhere she can. . . . And naturally she is the first to be searched. She is beaten, and the potatoes fall out one by one under the blows, in astounding amounts. The *Kapo*, crazy with anger when she sees the pile of potatoes that Helene dared to take, comes down on her even harder, and potatoes continue to fall out. It was like a Charlie Chaplin movie. We are all seized with nervous, crazy laughter that we try to hide. After the beating we begged Helene not to do it again. It would be the end of that idea!

"After about two months, there is a new selection. Instead of taking down the numbers of the skinniest girls and sending them to the gas chamber, the doctor starts writing down the numbers of the heaviest. After a long moment of doubt we realize that we are on the right side. I made it into the group. So it really is important for us to puff up our chest, and to pinch our cheeks so that they are rosy."

Misrepresent one's health under penalty of death, when one knows one is actually wasting away; "look smart," "look good" for your executioners: everything works as if the system itself was secreting these sadistic refinements, over and beyond the routine installments of regularly scheduled torture. . . . One can't help thinking how cruel the camp must be, along with the rest of it, for a child of fourteen to consider herself lucky to go to work in a factory!

Mala, Our Ideal!

"It is impossible to forget the prodigious story of Mala, which happened one evening in August of 1944, while we were still in Birkenau.

"The roll call is dragging on and on. The *Aufseherin* (the SS women guards) just won't stop counting and recounting our ranks. We can see they are in a panic about something. The reason why they are so upset finally becomes clear: 'It is Mala who is missing!' We are all overjoyed! Mala's reputation had spread throughout the camp. It seems certain to us that if Mala has succeeded in escaping, she will tell the whole world what we are going through, and people will come and rescue us! We cannot imagine for a moment that the great men of this world 'knew'!

"Mala is a young Jewish girl from Poland who arrived in September of 1942 in a shipment from Belgium. Very smart, and indeed gifted, she speaks five languages—Yiddish, Polish, Dutch, French, and German. At first she was an interpreter, then a *Laüferin,* a kind of messenger inside the camp, who would carry documents for the Germans from one part of the camp to another, which gave her access to the men's camp.

"Thanks to her extraordinary gifts, the SS came to trust her. She uses her influence to help us all, for changes in work assignments, among other things. She became a legend to all of us. We know her as 'Mala the Belgian.'

"Three or four weeks after her escape, again at evening roll call, we all notice that a gibbet has been set up in the yard. An SS guard is posted next to it. Some guards bring out Mala. We thought she had gotten away.

This appearance is the first we learn that she was caught. It is a dreadful shock! Mala whips out a razor that she has hidden in her clothing and begins to slash the artery in her wrist. The SS man tries to get the blade out of her hands. Mala strikes him with her bloody hand. She turns to us, shouting 'Be brave, the end is near!' Immediately, more guards come running and begin beating her. They are crazed, as if someone had directly defied them by making this unprecedented escape attempt. Mala will die in the cart that carries her toward the crematorium.

"After the war, we will learn that, during her errands inside the camp, she met a Pole who was not Jewish, a man named Edek. They fell in love. Edek worked as a plumber, which meant that he could go just about anywhere in the camp. It was thanks to other Polish prisoners and to a friend on the outside that their plan had gotten as far as it did. Alas, a patrol arrested them in the mountains of Zywiec and took them to the jail in Bielsko; from there they were brought back to Auschwitz, to the infamous Block number 11, reserved for torture.

"Mala's last moments have remained in the memory of each one of us as a symbol of courage that crushed us and sustained us the same time.

"Another drama within the larger one: at the time when the Hungarian Jews were arriving in July–August of 1944, the gypsies, who had all been parked near the Birkenau crematoria (about twenty thousand of them), were all gassed in the course of one night!"

The Factory

After the potato *kommando* came the factory.

"Although the working conditions were less harsh (closed hangars and some heat), the fact of working in the Union Werke armaments factory did not please us at all. But the French women who were working there when we arrived cheered us up by pointing out that 'it was not with a few of these hand grenades that Germany will win the war.' Instead of *kapos,* we have to deal with civilian foremen. The boss, Mr. Samson, sends the youngest of us, including me, to a table where we work sitting down. The work consists of adjusting springs in the Bakelite detonator inserts.

"We only learned later on that these were parts for hand grenades. The deportees who were assigned to quality control then tried to sabotage a batch of them, and serious sanctions followed. Here we did manage to talk a little, but very softly. We weren't beaten. We even had access to 'normal' toilets. Among other fortunate things, we probably owe it to this *kommando* that we survived!"

Did some detainees behave in a less group-spirited way than others, or do things you would criticize in retrospect?

Ida hesitates to answer. She wishes that it had not been the case. The truth is otherwise. But she refuses to sit in judgement. The circumstances were more than just "attenuating." But what use would it serve to pretend that "everyone was nice". . .

Story of a Gray Sweater

"It happened at the end of August, 1944. One day, when I was going to the bathroom, I passed a young Frenchman whom I recognized by the 'F' written on the star that identified him as a racial deportee (the Belgians wore a 'B,' the Dutch an 'H,' etc.). I had the feeling that I knew him from before, even with his shaved head. . . . Afterwards I remembered that he was the son of leatherworkers from Clichy who knew my parents.[15] His name came back to me, Jean G. I say to the girls who have jobs that put them in touch with the male prisoners to ask about the presence among them of one Jean G. Word comes back right away: 'It is indeed him, his father will be waiting for you tomorrow at nine o'clock at the break when the foremen have snack time.' (In the morning we never have any bread left, we ate it all the night before.)

"The next day, I mingled with the group that was mentioned, even though it was of course forbidden. A man with graying hair came toward me. His son had not told him the name of the deportee who had 'spotted' him. He was eager to know it. We both recognized each other."

"So it is really you, Ida? . . . Your father is looking for you."

"My father? Here? Suddenly I am dizzy. I have a knot in my throat. I who haven't cried, hardly, since I arrived in the camp, I dissolve in tears. I can't stop. I am incapable of asking him for how long my father has been there or where he is. Mr. G. is a little vague. My father has been here for a couple of weeks. He'll find me.

"The break ends and I am short on details. I return to my workbench. Still sobbing, I tell my comrades what is going on. They sympathize. Seeing me in tears nonstop, the foreman comes over and asks:

"*Was ist den loss?*" (What is going on?)

"Still sniffling, in my makeshift German, I explain to him that I have just learned that my father is in the camp, while I had thought he was at liberty in France. The foreman cuts me off":

"It is forbidden to cry. It makes the equipment rust!"

"I somehow can't manage to get control of myself. Now a woman supervisor shows up, and she asks me the same question. The foreman explains to her the reason for my sadness. Mr. Samson, the boss, now notices what is going on through the window of his office, and he comes out. It is his turn to ask:

"*Was ist den loss?*"

"I am incapable of answering him. The foreman tells him what is going on. The boss doesn't take a second to answer:

"Tell her to get me her father's number and I'll have him sent to the factory and she can see him."

"An almost 'human' response in what were fully inhuman circumstances. I am overwhelmed. Hope starts to return. Next morning I find father G. I tell him about the boss's promise. He shrugs his shoulders and says to me:

"Just think! Your father is a tailor, he could never work in the factory!"

"I realize the problem with this reasoning right away: Do you think that everyone who works here is a metal worker? Papa will be better off here than in an outdoors *kommando*.

"G. is not listening to me. When I see him several days later he does not give me my father's number. He tells me only that my father is cold and that he would like it if I could get him a sweater!"

"This is not a problem: I go directly to 'Canada,' the repository where people with privileges could choose from among the things confiscated from recent arrivals. A French girl who was a couple of years older than I (I met her after we returned from the camps but she made out that she didn't recognize me!) demands two rations of bread and one of margarine for a sweater. She could have probably just given me one, but ok! . . . What wouldn't I do to help my father! I pull together the goods for the trade. Some of my pals help me with a part of it from their own rations. It's all there. The following day, triumphant, I hand over to the father G. the fruit of our privations.

"The father G., whom I will never see again. Except out beyond the factory, wearing . . . the precious gray sweater!"

"The bastard," one wants to shout.

"It's not him I really am mad at, or the girl in 'Canada'; it's our executioners, for having pushed some of us to extremes they would not have reached on their own."

That is said without any posturing. Deliberately. Because it's obvious. Before going right on with what she was saying, as if to compensate for the overwhelming darkness of the picture with a dazzling show of light. Here it is.

A Crematorium Explodes

"It has often been said that no revolt was ever attempted in the camps: that's not true! There was the organized insurrection at Sobibor,[16] led by a Soviet officer in October of 1943, that enabled fifty men to escape and join the Bielorussian partisans. In Auschwitz it was more difficult. The SS and their dogs reacted immediately to the slightest breach of discipline. Few among us spoke Polish or German. That's why the revolt of the *Sonderkommandos* and the assistance provided by four women from the factory earned our admiration, and why its failure was so discouraging."

The *Sonderkommandos* are special work details, five or six hundred men, assigned to clear the bodies out of the gas chambers after gassing and to transport them in carts to the crematoria. So that they could not testify later, these men are themselves executed and replaced every three months. They know this going in. Doubtless they all hope that the war will end before their liquidation. In any case, they have no choice. If they refuse, they are killed immediately. We learned that some of them had to transport members of their own families. Very few of them survived.

Since they might just as well disappear, the idea came to them, during September of 1944, to blow up the entire gas chamber number 4. In order to do that, they needed some explosive. Some sympathizers got close to a group of Polish Jews working in the powder depot for the Union Werke factory. On October 7, the men in this revolt figured they had enough powder. The explosion happened, putting the crematorium out of commission.

Several hundred prisoners in this work detail were executed by firing squad. The guards had no trouble identifying the women who had helped provide the powder. Ida didn't forget a thing:

"A *kapo* came looking for them in the block, during October. We didn't know what had happened. The girls were tortured in the camp prison, in block 11.

"One evening in January 1945, the day shift that was just returning from work was ordered outside for a roll call. Right in front of us they had set up a gibbet with two nooses hanging at the ready. The commander of the camp himself, a Captain Bauer, made a long speech. He said, literally, 'If you obey, no harm will come to you. If you disobey, you see what awaits you.'

"We had to watch the hanging of two of the girls. The two others were executed in front of the night shift. This had a greater effect on me than everything else. We only learned afterwards what the girls had done. We were urged to watch the spectacle. I pretended to but looked away. The girls said nothing. They didn't have time to. But the sound of the rope going taut . . .

"A plaque on a wall in the Jewish block at Auschwitz commemorates their ordeal as does a stele at Yad Vashem in Jerusalem.[17] One reads their names: Ala Gertner, Roza Robota, Regina Safirstain, Estera Wajcblum. Without this act of revolt, our comrades would probably have survived, seeing as how they had made it that far. In November the Germans were going to blow up the other ovens, following orders from the SS to leave no trace of them. . . ." (This precaution proves, incidentally, that they were aware of wrongdoing, that they were afraid of being convicted of a crime!)

Another memory of the Union Werke: the visit, in 1944, of Heinrich Himmler, who was the top person in charge of the camps.[18] It was his second inspection of the camp. During the first, in 1942, he had said that the work of gassing prisoners wasn't going fast enough.

"The visit which I was present at was announced as an event, without our knowing exactly what the visitor did. We had to shine the facilities from bottom to top. A few days later the Nazi dignitary appeared, accompanied by at least ten officers. He didn't stop at our table. He went to inspect other divisions, probably the one where the grenades are finally assembled. When the group of officials passed in front of us, in a rustling of raincoats across the entire breadth of the aisle, I got the sinister feeling that a flock of crows had just passed. We lowered our heads in silence. I hardly saw him."

There is at least one other visit that Ida wants to mention, so strong a feeling of indignation it left her with.

"Let's not forget that the Red Cross visited Birkenau. We didn't see them because we were at work. But to this day it sticks in my throat. How could the delegation not have realized what was going on in the camp? Were they that naive? Why didn't they try harder to find out? No answer. Stunning silence."

An Incredible String of Lucky Breaks

What is it that made some people survive and others not? Ida is often asked this question when she speaks as a survivor in classrooms. There is no one single answer. Ida never stops repeating that she benefited from "unheard of breaks." What does this mean?

"First was the good luck to not get sick until after the evacuation of Auschwitz. If one had to go to the *Revier* one was done for! The constant attack on our morale drained away our strength in ways that are difficult to describe. It got worse as the humiliations added up: the mass latrines, the cold, the hunger, the insults. One doesn't get used to relieving oneself in front of everybody else, to never washing, to smelling bad, to being insulted from morning to night. The secret of our 'victory,' Geneviève de Gaulle said it very well, was to remain dignified at all costs, to not allow oneself to become dehumanized, and to resist together the systematic attempt to dehumanize us.

"My young age was a definite plus. At fourteen or fifteen years of age the instinct to survive is stronger than a few years later. Without even thinking about it, one hangs on. The fact of having left children back in France could give one added strength, but it also bore the risk of making one more discouraged. To lose spirit was the same as accepting to die in very short order. Without the will to hang in there, one began to slide, one crumbled. I believe that it must have been a lot harder for women of thirty or thirty-five years, already established in life, than for adolescents like me!"

Of course Ida never knew what it was like to be fourteen, fifteen, or sixteen and free as can be. Those years were stolen from her forever. But she is categorical about this:

"The strength one has during those years of life undoubtedly determined my survival."

"The Death March"

"January 18, 1945. It is winter and there is ice everywhere. We are coming back from our shift at the factory. We are given our usual rations. Suddenly the barrack leader announces the news: evacuation, we are going to leave, we don't know where to and under heavy guard, but Auschwitz is over and done with! I don't recall our celebrating. We have been misled for more than a year already. Was it not just another hoax?"

Ida and her friends did not know where the front lines were, neither those in the east nor those in the west. They had not heard that France had been entirely liberated, that General Leclerc had entered Strasbourg at the end of November,[19] and that Pétain and Laval had fled to Germany.[20] Brasillach was about to be executed.[21] The bombing of Dresden was days away, but they would not learn until much later how fate shifted in the War, how the traitors and the heroes would go down in History.[22] At the time, one thing was certain: they could hear artillery fire, over there, to the east. So it is the Russians, in principle, who were going to rescue them.

"Obviously, this fills us with joy. But experience had taught us to beware of false hopes. Are they going to blow us up along with the camp itself, as people were saying. Every passing hour brought its own surprises, its own pain. The truth is that the announcement of a mass departure sounded like the big turnaround that we were all waiting for.

Provided that the weakest among us can hold out for the time it takes for liberty to arrive!"

The Germans go around the *Reviers*, those pseudo-infirmaries where, while not being healed, the truly ill were relieved of having to work. Those who could still walk were ordered to rejoin blocks of "fit" detainees. Unfortunately some of the weakest among them decided to leave the *Revier* out of fear that the Germans were going to blow up the camp, and they did not have the strength for what was to follow.

The night was bright. Ida and her comrades stamp their feet in the glacial cold outside their barrack.

"Around ten or eleven o'clock at night, we leave. We are allowed to bring our blankets. I take one across my shoulders, but I will throw it away after our first stop."

"Why?"

"It was too heavy to carry."

To throw away this protection from the cold, which seemed so flimsy to them in their bunks, their strength must have seriously declined!

Some men tried to escape from the ranks, but Ida has no recollection that any women attempted this. Not speaking any Polish, they would have had little luck disappearing in the general population. Liliane left the infirmary with an active case of mumps despite the swollen glands that deformed her neck. By some miracle she didn't give out.

Leaving Auschwitz! In evoking this prodigious event, the act of using this verb and this noun together brings Ida the incredulous joy that they shared at that moment:

"Just imagine how utterly flabbergasting it is for us to pass under that famous gate announcing *Arbeit macht frei* again, and in a direction none of us hoped any longer we would, towards freedom. We have no idea what the immediate future will bring, what is waiting for us tomorrow, but the mere act of leaving the camp, lea-ving-the-camp!!!—fills us with an insane joy!

"I am wearing shoes that are too thin, that are too tight, which will lead to my getting frostbite, and the start of necrosis. The *kapos* have vanished. We are surrounded only by SS assisted by reservists from the

Wehrmacht. None of them tell us anything about where we are going. Basically, they are taking their labor force with them. Some of the strongest among us will work for them again following Auschwitz. Myself, I will be too sick to do so.

"If we slow down, the rifle butts start to come down on us. The women that fall are shot dead. The sides of the road are littered with corpses. One night we took shelter in a barn; one other night we found room in a stable where, I recall, a cow got loose. . . . We are not fed at all. I was lucky—lady Luck again—to go with my friend Fanny Weglieszewski, whose cousin had just brought her a loaf of bread just before the evacuation. For as long as I was with them, she shared that bread with Louise and me. Afterwards we got separated.

"I want to stress this detail. It has taken an enormous importance in my memories. It is possibly thanks to these small slices of bread that I survived at all!

"After that, there was only snow to fill our bellies. The girl on the outside of the rank grabbed a handful of it and passed it to us. We held up the ones who faltered. Despite the pain in my feet I kept walking like an automaton. It was 'walk or die'! This episode deserved the name of 'Death March,' since 50 percent of the people died along the way, from exhaustion, or by being shot. When a comrade began to weaken, we placed her in the middle of the rank and held her up, or hid her from the guards. We took turns.

"After walking 70 kilometers[23] in three days and three nights, we arrived in a city whose name I have forgotten.[24] There we are made to get onto gondolas, railroad cars with no roof, which were probably intended for transporting coal. We are even more tightly packed than in the convoy from Bobigny to Auschwitz. Many can't even sit down. I managed to, but fights break out over space. We are at the end of our strength, and of our nerves. Some women 'blow their fuses,' as we say today. The only upside of the lack of a roof: during the two day–plus trip to Ravensbrück,[25] we have nothing to eat, we have to be happy opening our mouths to catch falling snow."

Stopover in Ravensbrück

"We arrive in Ravensbrück around the 25th or 26th of January. We will leave again on February 15. The camp is overcrowded, disorganized. Several women's camps had been evacuated there. They had set up an enormous tent. Many women slept right on the ground. I find myself in a solid barracks, I don't know why.

"We do not work. Typhoid fever is sweeping through the camp. My toes have lesions everywhere. I can hardly walk. If I had been in this condition during the 'March,' I wouldn't have made it, my life would have ended by the roadside. I am waiting to see what will happen next, the only French girl around.

"Another stroke of luck, this one highly improbable: the SS's confusion led to our being shipped off to Neustadt in passenger cars.[26] We are no longer packed in. I remember one girl was singing. These conditions help us to regain a bit of our morale, although I had lost all of my old girlfriends. I can no longer recall any of the women I made this last trip with. The March and hunger had turned us all into zombies. And still—these coincidences are not so rare, in all the moving about—I saw the sisters I mentioned earlier once more.[27] Régine and Claudine have disappeared. I will only be reunited with Liliane and Claudine in Neustadt.

"When we arrived in Neustadt, we were placed in some kind of barn. This is where I came down with typhus. I am delirious all night long.

I can't stand. Liliane takes me to the *Revier*. It is full to capacity. The following day we try again at the *Revier*. A woman died in the night. Her place is now available and, a new miracle, the Polish nurse who is going to do everything she can to save me is called Wanda!"

The Miracle of Miracles

Another miracle, the most astonishing of all: the arrival of Wanda. She makes her appearance at the *Revier* of Neustadt, where Ida stayed, from February 14th to May 2nd, 1945. Ida's feet were partially frozen during the Death March. Any more and she would certainly have fallen by the wayside where she would have received the treatment reserved for the weakest. Ida explains:

"In the infirmary, we don't work, but nobody cares for us. We are abandoned between life and death. Was the gangrene going to take the entire foot? Suddenly a Polish nurse wearing the red triangle for political prisoners leans over me. (I will later learn that she was an active resister in the Polish secret army and that she continued to lead a clandestine existence under the Soviet occupation, which would earn her 'seconds' in the communist prisons!)

"At first all I see is her hair-bun. She had somehow avoided having her head shaved. I had forgotten what normal hair looked like. For me it means freedom. Wanda—I only knew her by her first name—does not speak French. But I am good at learning foreign languages. On the assembly line in the Union Werke factory I worked side by side with some Polish Jewish women, who taught me. I still remember some bits of Polish. We share our feelings, and very soon we become fast friends."

With precious skills and knowledge she had acquired working for an orthopedist, Wanda starts to care for Ida. She alternates hot and cold baths to stimulate renewed circulation. She gets some potassium permanganate to enhance the effect of the baths. She improvises bandages with strips of paper. Ida describes her rescue with such grateful emotion as if it had all happened yesterday:

"Wanda finds what she can to feed me. Since I can't swallow dark, hard bread, she makes me eat potato soups prepared by her colleagues with fried onions in them. She requires me to eat. She uses motherly strictness: 'If you want to go back home, she repeats, you absolutely must eat!' In short, she saves my life!

"Typhus is now making me delirious. I am told that, while unconscious, I say things in Polish. I recall shouting out 'Vive la France!'[28] At first, Liliane came to see me, but soon the epidemic was so bad that they isolated the *Revier* where I was from the camp itself. No one could come near it. Which caused an end to the visits as well as a delay in our being released.

"Another unimaginable break: among all of the unknown women, I find my old friend Claudine. She is on the top level of the bunk opposite mine. I am on the bottom. I have no idea how long she has been there. She doesn't know herself. She has a freshly shaved head, like me, no doubt because of typhus. We were all covered with lice, and it was them that transmitted it. Finding each other like this made us both extremely happy. We would be repatriated in the same airplane. Death alone could separate us, and it finally did, several years ago now.

"My lucky streak continued right up to my liberation. Because the camp in Neustadt was in Germany and not in Poland, it had no gas chamber. There were no selections. There was moreover the unexpected assistance of Wanda in the *Revier*. And now Claudine! If I had caught typhus two months earlier, I would have been done for.

"On April 30, 1945, the Germans all fled. The 'girls' found themselves all alone in a deserted camp, where many of us remained from February 14 until May 2. At this point we were condemned to remain there, bedridden, waiting for we knew not what! Claudine, who could see everything from high up on her bed, spotted the Germans burning the camp archives before heading off. Wanda said good-bye to them, and then she too disappeared. The camp was abandoned, and there was nothing left behind to eat. Captivity without bars or jailers. Time seemed to have stopped!"

"Hello!"

"Suddenly, on May 2nd exactly (we never forgot what date it was, in the back of our minds!), I raise my eyes, looking out of my lower bunk, and I see . . . three American soldiers! In my memory, they are huge, one meter eighty-five or ninety centimeters.[29] They are wearing caps, and their uniforms look like they just emerged from the dry cleaner's. We stare at them, transfixed. They are magnificent. They seem surprised to find us here, and by the way we look."

"'Hello!' say the soldiers.

"'Hello!' we answer.

"The conversation ends there. The soldiers don't know a word of French, nor we a word of American. Not a doctor among them. They are reconnoitering. In their expressions we see astonishment turn into compassion faced with the children that we are—eighteen- and fifteen-year-olds, the last fifteen months of which spent in the camps! Their first move was to empty their pockets of the chewing gum and chocolates that had come in their rations. After which they leave as they had come, without another word.

"We believe that they are going to inform their commanders, to see help that will arrive right away. It didn't happen like that. A day went by, then the morning of the next, without anyone coming back. Emboldened by her ability to walk (not like me—still flattened by my exanthematic typhus), my bunk-mate, a resister named Ginette, decides that since the

Germans have left and the Americans are not taking care of us, she is going to get help herself.

"She goes to the town of Neustadt-Glewe, which fortunately is only two kilometers away.[30] There she runs into some Russian soldiers who had just arrived. Without realizing it, we were located exactly at the spot on the Elbe River where the Americans and the Soviets met up. Ginette manages to make these latter understand mostly by sign language that there are sick people to rescue; and in the afternoon I saw Russians arrive equipped with large . . . wheelbarrows."

Ida is not a little proud. For once, she almost brags:

"Not everybody could claim this distinction: I can say with pride that I was liberated in a wheelbarrow!"

The Russians install the girls in a requisitioned hospital, from which they watch come out—without much feeling of pity, Ida adds—German soldiers on crutches, covered with bandages.

"We get royally installed in private rooms. The first thing that really warms my heart is having sheets on the bed. This is a luxury unknown since my arrest. The first sensation of liberty is this clean bedding! Perhaps it was luck, again, to be liberated by the Russians, rather than by the British, because I later learned that some of my comrades died from being fed corned beef too soon and they died of it, from dysentery. Doubtless the Russians had already had to take care of other prisoners. They have the experience needed to return us slowly to a normal diet, feeding us soups that were progressively less clear, cereals, supplements, and vitamin shots.

"After approximately three weeks they asked the French women, the Belgian, and the Dutch to sign up to be shipped home in the coming days. I sign up, and then all of a sudden it occurs to me that Claudine, who is in a room that is isolated from the rest of us (because she was still sicker than we), will perhaps not have heard about this repatriation. I decide to go and tell her about it, but I can't stand up yet. So I crawl on my butt along the tiled floors of the hospital, and I make progress by small sliding movements. Claudine welcomes me with joy and thanks me for this good news.

"They certainly would have found her in the end, but I was afraid that she hadn't found out soon enough. I was determined that we would return home together! She will remember the story and will tell the story to her grandchildren, who would see it as a tremendous feat. For them, I will always be the woman 'who saved granny'!"

After an additional week in the Russian zone,[31] and a suitable diet, the girls are offered the opportunity to leave in trucks. They refuse as one, with the ferocity of a stalked beast. For them, trucks are the embodiment of everything threatening:

"Trucks? Not on your life!

"The soldiers try to reassure us: the war is over, there is nothing left to fear. We accept to go via road to Lunebourg, in the French/British zone. A French doctor proposes to put us in a hospital in Germany. Claudine and I both start crying like the babies that we are. We beg to return to France. It seems to us both that we really won't be out of harm's way until we cross back over the border.

"Return via train? The French doctor is not in favor of that: given my condition, I might not survive the trip, which has taken some people as long as two weeks during which some of my comrades had perished. But, instead, he promises that the first available space on board an aircraft will be ours. That very evening—again, a real bit of luck!—an empty military plane is set to leave for le Bourget.[32] It was a Dakota that belonged to the Canadian army. We are loaded on board on stretchers, wearing clothes I can no longer remember, given to us by the Russians, and a turban to hide our shaved heads."

“Revoir Paris”[33]

During the flight, another memorable moment: a steward leans over Ida and offers her a cigarette, a Player’s.

“Cigarette, Miss?”

“Despite my fifteen years, which I had grown used to hiding from myself, I accept like a grown up, playing the part of a young woman. After the first drag I can barely keep from throwing up.

“An hour later, two hours perhaps (planes didn’t travel very fast in those days), the same steward comes out of the pilot’s cabin to announce that we have crossed the border, that we are flying over France. That moment has remained magical, intense, overwhelming.

“This time is really it, it is truly Freedom! We have it in our grasp, no one is going to take it away from us now! I remember the line by Victor Hugo[34]: ‘One has to experience exile to truly love France!’ In 1947, when Charles Trénet will sing ‘*Revoir Paris*, just a little one month’s stay . . . ,’ and every time I hear the three happy notes *do re mi*, I get teary eyed thinking about the steward saying in his Canadian accent: ‘We are flying over France!’”

Ida recaps her experience:

“My liberation, my return to lost humanity, can be summed up in this way: clean sheets in the Russian zone, at last men who were ‘normal,’ whom one might imagine wanting to kiss, a drag of blonde tobacco that makes your head spin, and a glimpse of France, there, between two clouds, beneath the wings of a Dakota.”

First Antibiotics

The challenge faced by the deportees was not a one-day affair for any of them. The complications were sometimes fatal, and often quite slow. For Ida they would be both medical and familial, in both cases atrocious. She explains:

"At le Bourget, because ours was not a regularly scheduled flight, no one was waiting for us. We didn't get full military honors with the playing of *La Marseillaise*[35] that accompanied the arrival of the other returnees. But the shock of returning to France was so great that Claudine felt unwell right there on the tarmac.

"On arrival, a doctor refused to let me go home to try and find my parents, my brother. 'You will write,' he orders me, and he has me checked in at the Hôpital Broussais, where I would stay for two months.

"I am barely checked in when Claudine arrives by ambulance from the Hôpital Bichat, where there was no more room. We exploded with joy to be together again, as if by another miracle. They put us in beds side by side in a very large room where there were a dozen other returnees from Germany. A nurse picks me up in her arms and carries me there. Naively, I ask if I am not too heavy.

"'Oh no, little one!' she says, and her eyes fill up with tears. Despite one entire month of carefully administered food in the Russian zone, I must still only weigh thirty-some kilos.[36] The nurse immediately gives me a bath in a real bathtub, the first I had in such a long time! The gentle heat fills my body. What a delight! We dreamed about them often. It was what we all wished for first when we thought about coming home . . .

"In the course of a full follow-up medical visit, the doctor questions me about the consequences of my feet having been frozen. He confirms that the care my feet had been given by Wanda in Neustadt was indeed the best possible, without which I would certainly have had to have them amputated."

A Hat with Cherries on It

"The next morning, I get a pneumatic message[37] sent to my brother, and a telegram to Alice, my host mom in Lié. My brother works nights at the PX, the American Army stores.[38] He comes to the hospital immediately. At the entrance to the ward, he looks around for me, but doesn't see me. I call out:

"'That's my brother, he doesn't recognize me!'

"Nurses and patients start to cry, when they realize that I have become unrecognizable by my nearest and dearest. The same scene occurs every time families appear and have the same difficulty finding each other.

"My brother comes over. He is speechless. He doesn't ask me any questions. He only says that our parents have not come back. This doesn't keep me from hoping, for a very long time, that my father would eventually return.

"Alice answers my telegram right away asking me if I can come and visit her soon. I explain to her that I must first undergo surgery. Impatient, she decides to come up to Paris, which she had never ever done in her life!"

Alice arrives, dressed in black, wearing a straw hat. "With cherries on it!" Ida recalls. The farm woman from Lié stands still in the doorway to the community room. She looks around at all the patients, hesitating. She doesn't recognize her little protégée either. It is Ida who has to call to her:

"Alice! I'm over here. It's me!

"Alice rushes to my bedside letting out a cry whose intensity does not hide her strong country accent:

"'My dahh-ling Idaah!'

"The entire room shared in our reunion, with laughter mixed with tears. Claudine never forgot the apparition of the country woman in her Sunday best and her wild 'My dahh-ling Idaah!'

"The hospital allowed us to eat what we wanted. Often we would wake up at night to have a snack. We fattened up like little pigs. Claudine's uncles expressed their concern about this to the head doctor. He answered them with a lack of concern that left me wondering:

"'Let them be! Who knows how long they are going to survive!'

"We got the impression that our return upset them somehow.

"I got in touch with my uncle and aunt in Clamart, the Dembskis. They come to see me, along with my two cousins. They survived, along with my cousin the leather worker—the maker of the little bag that my father had given me that was taken from me when I arrived at the camp. His wife and their son escaped too. Although the visits from these survivors lifted my spirits, they also made me feel more acutely the non-return of my mother and my father.

"Despite the kilos I have gained, I am still very thin. My cousin Régine comforts me, squeezing my slender wrist, with a wise saying translated from Yiddish:

"'Where there are bones, there will be flesh!'"

The doctor on duty refuses to sign off on the mastoid operation: he thinks that Ida is too weak. But the surgeon overrules him and proceeds. This is fortunate because a mastoid infection was starting. To combat the postoperative infection they would use penicillin, which was just coming on the market. To all of Ida's lucky breaks must be added this progress in antibiotics, just in time!

Towards the end of July, following a bout of pleurisy, the doctors say they want to send Ida to the mountains to convalesce. The social worker puts her in touch with a colleague at the ADIR, the association of deported members of the Resistance founded by Geneviève de Gaulle when she returned from Ravensbrück.[39] Even though they were not resisters, the ADIR takes both Ida and Claudine into their care, as well as their new friend, Hélène.[40]

Learning about the Resistance

Ida gets identification papers and a passport. The photo for it is the first one taken of her following her return, with hair that has just barely begun to grow back. She is offered a stay in Switzerland, in Montana.[41] Her cousin Régine recommends the place. Ida is also eager to visit Switzerland.

"I start thinking about the mountains," she says, "the chocolate!

"I will remain there for fourteen months, coddled. As far as comfort is concerned, it was a dream! We lived in individual villas. We ate good meals. The ambiance was ideal. I met lots of girls there who were to become close friends: Charlotte Delbo, Anne Baron, Anise Girard, who would become Anise Postel-Vinay, and Francoise Zavadil.[42] An Englishwoman who was there caring for her son gave us English lessons. I was avoiding thinking about the problem of my future. It was Anne who thought about this the most.

"One day, two men came from the Joint, an American organization that helped Jews in difficulty the world over.[43] They gave us pocket money. Towards the end of our stay, they proposed to send me to prepare for a career in the hotel industry at a school in Zurich. But I wanted to return to France. I should have asked them for advice, maybe some addresses. I didn't consider the possibility that I might undertake studies at a university, which Madame Picard always said I had the intelligence for. Here I was seventeen with only a diploma from primary school!

"Deportation miraculously left me with my life, but it ruined my chances of entering a profession that matched my full potential."

Even the Dog . . .

Just what was the reception like, in France, after her sixteen months of detention in the camp, plus the time spent in Switzerland? Ida recalls with great clarity the mood of the country at the time:

"At the end of 1946, deportation was thought to be a thing of the past. People talked about it even less than they did forty years later. There was no way to reenter the school system. I came back to live with my brother, without having completed the studies that might have opened other doors to me."

Today, when the slightest accident gives a person access to psychological support, all kinds of specialists and agencies would be available to a young woman of seventeen returning from an experience like Auschwitz. At the time this was not yet even on the horizon; people simply didn't expect it.

"Not the shadow of a psychologist! Our physical health was looked after, but nobody paid attention to anything else."

The reception in Sompt, when Ida returned for the first time, in 1947, brought some consolation, even if it didn't do anything for her future.

"The whole village and my classmates throw a party. Even the little dog named Gardienne, that I hadn't seen in three years, jumps up on me as if we had only been apart since yesterday. Her performance has everyone in tears. Her memory and her effusive greeting set a good lesson in fidelity to the human onlookers."

Everything else is left unsaid. There is no mention of what has become of the two policemen who arrested Ida, nor of her future schooling or of a career. Monsieur Poupinot, the mayor, has suffered a stroke. Life is just getting back to normal. Gardienne's affections captured the lime-light. Ida will experience some of these feelings again in 1996 when Jean-Marie Pouplain, a historian and a corresponding scholar with the Institute for History of the Present Time, along with the then-mayor, Claudette Grelier, will organize a surprise meeting with her former schoolmates. Despite the half-century that had passed, Ida will be proud of herself for having recognized every one of them!

That same day, a classmate of Ida from the dark years[44] will present Ida with her little ruler from school that was saved when the house in Lié was sold. This will be the occasion for a pilgrimage to the chapel in Sompt where Alice had had a statuette of the Virgin installed along with a plaque that reads: "Thanks to Mary—1945," in fulfillment of a vow she made if her devotions to the Virgin would "bring" Ida back from the camps. Although not a believer, Ida had in fact told herself, in the darkest hours of her deportation, that maybe Alice's prayers were protecting her. In 2001, while visiting the scene again in preparation for writing her memoirs, Ida will not fail to visit the chapel where Alice spent so many hours thinking about her . . .

Alice's Demise

Life gets under way again. In 1953 Ida marries, and from Fensterzab, she becomes Ida Grinspan. Both she and her husband work from home. When Ida travels to Sompt, she will do so alone. Alice is disappointed, and Ida noticed:

"Alice thinks my husband didn't come out of pride. Alice is a very touchy person, easily offended. She already suffered from depression before the war. Her memory is poor. She frequently says, 'I am so scatterbrained, I am so scatterbrained!'

"There have been a lot of deaths in the Marché family. Alice lost her second husband right after the war, from leukemia. Her brother Charles, who was also a close friend to me, died suddenly, as did their mother and grandmother. After the war, as early as 1947, the first time I returned to Lié, Alice asked me to stay with her. She told me that the township had decided to grant me the same pension as its veterans who were returning prisoners of war. She hoped that I would settle nearby. But my mother had made me promise to 'not remain in the countryside.'

"One morning in 1954, when I was living near the avenue Gambetta, one of Alice's aunts calls me up. She was the wife of a police officer. She tells me that Alice has tried to take her own life with some medicine. She goes on: 'Only you can boost her morale.'

"I put down my needle, which is how tailors say 'I dropped everything,' and I went out there. I spent several days with Alice. She had not really recovered from her suicide attempt. She had the impression that her neighbors were laughing behind her back. She thought that she was damned to hell, excommunicated. I reminded her that the church put its trust in divine mercy. I swore to her that no one was making fun of her or judged her. At the time it seemed like she was improving. When I returned home I told my husband that I thought I had brought her some comfort.

". . . Several days later, at eleven at night, a phone call from Alice's aunt Juliette: 'This time Alice didn't miss, she hanged herself!'

"I didn't go to her funeral because of her distant relatives whom I didn't want to see. I regretted it. For her sake, of course, but also because I would have gotten some personal things back, if only the little note from my mother, or my yellow stars. I only have one memento of my life in Lié: a little wooden school ruler that I had written my name on, which a classmate returned to me in 1996."

The former top student in the school in Sompt shows the precious token of a time when misfortune didn't yet exist. It resembles all such school-day vestiges. Signed "Ida" on each of its four sides, with scratches and traces of purple ink, it looks like it was used to underline a lot of homework.

Looking at it, one can almost hear the squeaking of chalk on the board, and the shouts of recess, the carefree happiness from before the cataclysm . . .

"Slog"

Ida remembers the period following the war as a "slog," even if that isn't how people ordinarily characterized it. No help was provided. The right to some kind of pension was not granted until later. For Ida this would come in 1956.

"I helped my brother with his very 'do it yourself' dressmaking business. I made deliveries. My uncle and aunt in Clamart offered to let me stay with them, but I dreaded being considered the 'poor cousin.' I have always had my pride. It's about all that I did have, and I hung on to it. I preferred to live from hand to mouth even if some days there wasn't anything to eat at all. I didn't go out in the evening much. I took tests to get into an intensive course at a secretarial school . . . which never opened.

"Dressmaking represented an immediate solution to my problems. I didn't know the OSE yet,[45] the agency for helping children, which saved many Jewish kids during the Occupation, and which took care of orphans following France's Liberation. No one ever helped me, as they did my friend from the potato *kommando,* whom the OSE guided into studies to become a social worker. I missed out on what opportunities there were. Yes, deportation didn't just threaten to put our lives in danger: it also denied many of us our chance to succeed.

"I thought about the camp a lot following my return, although only when I was alone. People did not want to hear about it. Associations of survivors were less active than they became later on. The Auschwitz Survivors Friendship Society existed,[46] but it was far from where I lived. At the end of January, we celebrated the opening of the camp among ourselves.

"It was time to move on."

A Certain Leo

The legal fallout from the camps—Ida never paid much attention to this. Given that the trials of the Germans and their accomplices would not give her back her parents, whose disappearance was her greatest sadness, her concern for truth, equity, vengeance, or reparation was nonexistent. All she knew was the boundless contempt she felt for the torturers with whom she had had to deal.

One day in 1947, however, the past and the fate of the torturers demanded her involvement in the form of a call to be a witness. Ida was summoned to the Quai des Orfèvres.[47]

The inspector checked her papers, and confirmed the record of her stay in the various camps. He asks her a question:

"Did you ever meet one Klara Pfortsch?"

Ida had no memory of such a person. The policeman clarifies:

"She was a *kapo*."

"There were so many of them," Ida replies.

"She was known as Leo," the inspector adds.

Ida jumps. This is a different story. "Leo" was well known. For her violence, her sadism. Ida described her: hair cut short like a tomboy, very masculine, a raincoat down to the ankles like the SS, a stick in her hand, a very distinctive way of beating the girls, throwing them head and shoulders to the ground. "She was certainly a lesbian," said the prisoners. Possible, but "Little" Ida didn't even know what the word meant.

The policeman went on: "Leo" was being held by the Russians. France was calling for her extradition so that she could be put on trial in their zone. If they get her, and if her trial takes place, would Ida accept to appear in court as a witness and repeat her testimony in front of the tribunal? She answers "yes"; without any sense of bitterness, but without any hesitation either.

Several months later she receives the order from the army to go to Germany. As luck would have it, still at work, her friend Claudine had received the same summons. So they travel together to Rastatt. They are lodged with local residents. Deposition in front of the tribunal of the armed forces occupying Germany, October 6, 1949. It is indeed "Leo" who is in the dock, minus the swagger she had had back in the camp.

"Do you recognize her?" the witnesses are asked.

"Without a doubt!"

Klara, aka Leo, had a good lawyer. He pleaded attenuating circumstances, stating that his client had been arrested because she was a communist, that she had been made bitter by having been imprisoned for four or five years. "Not so!" protests Ida, years later: the especially fearsome *kapo* wore a black triangle indicating that she was imprisoned as "asocial," and not the red triangle worn by political prisoners. The verdict: death! Ida notes:

"That we recognized her, absolutely, without evident hatred but unwaveringly, that must have impressed the tribunal!"

Get Even? What Good Would That Do?

In fact, the sentence was commuted. The condemned woman was out in twelve years. The news reached the survivors' association.

"What effect did that have on you? Did you still have the feeling that you wanted to get even with 'Leo'?"

"Honestly, I only felt disgusted indifference."

"What about towards the police officers from Melle?"

"I don't know how to answer that. I am by nature not a hater. What could a girl of sixteen or seventeen do to them, following Liberation? Get a gun? Go and shoot all three of them? It didn't come naturally to me. I was already against the death penalty, more than thirty years before it was actually abolished.[48]

"Quite frankly, life in a concentration camp breaks you. And you stay that way if you come back alone, without your parents. It didn't matter that I was young and that I wanted to live 'despite everything,' something inside me had been destroyed, and it could not be fixed. What vengeance? What good would that do me! An enormous contempt for those sick creeps was all I felt. It was so huge, what I had gone through because of them! How could they possibly have had no remorse? You can't teach people to be ashamed, that's for sure!"

Ida reconsiders: the French officer thanks to whom a girl of fourteen was thrown into a cattle car heading for a fate that was perfectly well known to him did not deserve her resentment, but still:

"I think I would have a few questions I'd like to ask him."

At this thought, Ida's face suddenly revealed a steely coldness that she had never shown during the entire time we worked together.

Antigone

A meeting between Ida and the captain of the police who arrested her almost really occurred.

This was in the early 1970s. Ida was idly watching television. The program was a documentary and a debate about UFOs and other "apparitions," a subject that was very popular at the time, pitched to the broadest audience imaginable.

A group of "experts" was gathered on the set in the studio, chosen as broadcasters usually do by their popular culture credentials: most of them had published a book on the subject. This was the case with a certain Émile T., author of *Sur la Piste de l'homme inconnu*, published by Amiot-Dumont in 1951.[49] This man made Ida feel uneasy, but nothing more than that.

Suddenly, as Mr. T. introduced himself as a retired police officer in the Poitou, Ida jumped. The man's face had said something to her, but now it became clear, and the memory popped out at her: this man was none other than the captain to whom she had refused to give her father's address in 1944 and who sent her to Auschwitz via Drancy! He was indeed the officer who had been patiently waiting for the "Jewish girl from Lié" back at the police station of the Sub-Prefecture.[50] He must have been the officer who considered her to be both harmful and dangerous, since he had sent three of his subordinates to arrest a girl of fourteen. He who wittingly planned to send her to extermination (we do recall one of the accomplices assuring Alice: "You'll never see her again!").

Ida hasn't the slightest doubt. By this time the events were twenty-five years old, but time does not erase images, especially not of such highly charged situations. If someone had said to her that memories fade, as the lawyers of French collaborators with the Nazis often did, she could well have answered that at her age, as at any age, to be awakened in the middle of the night and subjected to questions of life and death, that carves out a memory that lasts forever. How could Ida have forgotten the way her sixteen months of slow death began, and how it could have been avoided: being torn away from the Marché family farm which had become "her" home, being driven under armed guard to Melle, the police officer's office, the portrait of the "good Marshal" on the wall, and the urgent questions, the threats, the extortion!

What Ida could not say herself, she being too modest and too much involved to do that, we have to imagine for ourselves as if we were overhearing that conversation in 1944 from behind a door. The face-off is worthy of an ancient tragedy. On one side: a forty-year-old officer, the zealous representative of Vichy France's policy of law and order in the service of the Occupation in its hunt for the Jewish population of Europe; on the other a teenager of that people refusing adamantly to give up her own! A little slip of an Antigone standing up to the grumpy Creon from the so-called humanistic country known as France![51]

Ida's thought in 1970 is to reach for the telephone. She calls the television network where her executioner is strutting his stuff. The "Jewish girl from Lié" knows how to make herself heard when she puts her mind to it; it is precisely this strength of character that saved her life. She gets the switchboard of the program on the line. She shows the same aplomb as when she was fourteen, encouraged by the policeman's own boldness.

"You are talking about 'the walking dead,' and that works for me: I am one of the 'walking dead.' I have a word or two to say to Mr. T.

"Who are you?'"

"'The walking dead,' I'm telling you."

She had no idea what she would have said if they had put her through to the studio, to talk to the man who was responsible for having sent her off to hell, where she had by a miracle survived. Would she have asked him why he hadn't pretended to the Germans that the "Jewish girl" had escaped or that the vehicle had broken down as Madame Picard had suggested, and as was often done? To this day she says she has no idea what she would have done. Her feeling with regard to the policemen in Melle has not changed since the moment when they appeared in Alice's home: nothing that could be done to them would return her parents to her—all she cared about—what she feels is absolute contempt for them more than anger.

Be it true or false—we will never know—the television studio's reply saved Émile T. from what might have been an unpleasant moment:

"We're not broadcasting live," came the reply.

Technology covers up for a lot. In this case it deprived us of a historic dialogue, a moment of truth.

Ida regrets nothing. Good pen-pusher for the barbarians that he was, Mr. T. did not deserve her enmity, much less her active attention. Too bad for him if team spirit had taken the place of his having a soul! Too bad for him if he had never been awakened in the middle of the night, as Ida was, by a whiff of his own remorse! Orders from on high shielded him from any dishonor. He has certainly departed this world by now. His descendants who bear his name have every right to be left out of it. Which is why we have only used the initial.

But after what Ida went through, and what we have just read, it is not inconceivable that third parties might seek to clarify what happened, in her place if not in her name, including the manner in which those orders were carried out, and how they might not have been. Or as compared to how the *Épuration* functioned—much more leniently than is commonly believed.[52]

"The Policemen Could Have Saved Her"

"There exists in every hierarchical state agency an unbroken chain of authority that is at the same time a chain of responsibility."

This observation made at Nuremberg[53] by Edgar Faure, an assistant prosecutor, is mentioned by Jean-Marie Pouplain as an epigraph to *Les Chemins de la honte* (Geste Editions, 2000),[54] a very thorough inquiry into the persecution of Jews in the Deux-Sèvres, of which Ida's arrest was a part.

Following the arrests in 1942, the department, in principle, contained no more Jews other than the French ones who, thanks to the UGIF, thought they were safe. The roundup on January 31, 1944, put an end to that illusion. A few fortunate ones were not arrested at that time: out of 108 whose presence was known, only 70 were arrested, and 58 of those were transferred to the camp in Poitiers.[55] Among them, there were 18 young people and children, including Ida.

The root of the crime which is seen to be against humanity: a German order, which, if it hadn't been given, one can always hope the French authorities would not have chosen to carry out—to pursue the persecution of the Jews, although as we know the statute of October 1940 actually took the lead in some respects.[56] We are referring to the order given by Nazi Security police chief Karl Herold on January 27, 1944, to all prefects in the departments of Charente, Charente-Maritime, Vendée, Deux-Sèvres, and Vienne to arrest all of the Jews remaining in their jurisdictions. The reason given: the Jews were supposedly "involved" in terrorist acts carried out by communists and groups opposed to the Germans.

The confidential instructions are enough to make one sick: the operation must be carried out on January 31 at 3 a.m., in order to avoid "incidents." Families were to be arrested together, without regard to the age of the children. Destination: Drancy, in closed transport vehicles. Baggage permitted: warm clothing, food for three days; do not neglect to bring money and any valuables (they will soon learn what thievery this is intended to facilitate!).

A clear paper trail tells the tale: the prefects relayed the order to local and state chiefs of police, with the names and addresses of people to arrest, and an endless number of discretionary measures in case the local population reacted badly. They ordered the necessary buses, which were to be standing by in Niort starting at midnight.

The warrant for the operation that took place in Lié was signed by the three policemen from the brigade in Melle that came to announce to "the Jewess Fensterzab, Ida" her arrest with a view to internment. As if to clear itself of any wrongdoing, the warrant specifies—which Ida contests—that the aforementioned had "become aware of the order of the German authorities" that required her to go with them, and that she consented to doing this following a search for weapons that turned up none.

The immediate protests of Alice Marché, of the mayor of Sompt, and of the schoolteacher Madame Picard went unheard, as did the later attempt by Alice to intervene with the local German authorities. Starting at the railway station in Poitiers, in Drancy, and at Bobigny, the vast machine to crush, to dehumanize and to exterminate, is set to work.

It was not until after the Liberation of France that the conduct of the policemen would be exposed to the light of day by several investigations, coming from different directions.

Starting in October of 1944, the "Purification Committee" in Melle brings up what it continues to call—the vocabulary at least has resisted time—"the matter of the Jewess in Sompt." Out of the three people in the area that were to be visited in the night of January 30—31, the Committee notes that two, living in La Mothe, were warned by people they knew in the prefecture, proof that administrative subversion was possible. They only found Ida.

"In this painful business," the Committee finds that responsibility lies particularly with the Germans who gave the order, an order that was "impossible not to deliver," and "difficult to not execute." The duty to disobey the inhuman was not mentioned. As for how it was done, the "Chief B." might have been "quite clumsy, not to say hard." The Committee still had not heard Madame Picard's testimony.

She appears in front of the Committee on October 17. Ida's teacher summed up her testimony in her written report to her school inspector. She is surprised that Ida's uncles and cousins in Clamart, on the outskirts of Paris, escaped being arrested, thanks to tips from some policemen, while Ida, out in the boondocks, was unable to benefit from such protection. Madame Picard clearly gives in to righteous indignation:

> What sense can you make of the fact that in a big city the Jews are saved, while in the countryside they are snatched from us? And what must one think of a brigade of the state police that, once it found out that she was Jewish, turned its attention to arresting this child?
>
> 1) In order to discredit the poor child in this matter, the police tried to connect her with the writing of an anonymous letter (apparently her handwriting is similar! . . .) Quite surprisingly the inquiry was dropped. . . . The police only left the girl alone when Miss V.[57] told them that the girl was beyond suspicion. So their attempt failed.
>
> 2) They returned several times in order to demand that this poor girl wear the Jewish badge,[58] but the mayor himself, as well as I, had forbidden her to do this. That shows how much concern there was, in the township of Melle, for this one child! We did not want to lose her, you understand. I don't know who deserves the blame for this, but what I do know is that the man in charge did nothing to save her, quite the contrary, I think, as I have just explained to you, that the matter was carefully thought out in advance.
>
> Having nobody but this poor little girl to protect from danger, her case was made even more precarious by failing to get her papers in order. From the shepherd girl that she was, she was handed over as a student. The child protested. So she was put in with a bunch of old people, in order to get rid of her more quickly, no doubt . . .

In order to make matters clear, our mayor had the child's certificate of French nationality carried over to the captain by the same policemen, so that he would understand that he was handing over a little French girl, but nothing could deter such a great chief, who could simply have said: "Cancel the child's ration card (which would have been easy enough since it was the end of the month in the night of the 30th to the 31st of January) and say she no longer lives here!" Would our town not have fed her? Didn't we already save an English family in this way? Just this small suggestion to make!

Well, if he had really wanted to save her, all he would have to have done is to let the air out of the car tires and while the policemen took care of that he could send a van around. We all would have hidden the girl. Myself I had always said to her, "If you are ever in danger, try to get free and come to our house." Since this arrest, the police have sensed the disapproval of the community, and the policemen and the adjutant have all said that Lié will pay dearly for it following the war. And why is that? It's because people don't just say "bravo!" after witnessing such a cowardly act.

Dear Mr. Inspector, I have said just about everything that I had on my mind. I gave a deposition last Thursday, but I was not able to say all that I thought. I think that I have said everything succinctly so that you can judge for yourself and so that you can have the satisfaction of participating in the triumph of Justice.

Mr. Inspector, excuse me for bothering you but I also want to say that nothing will deter me, especially as since last Saturday I have reason to believe that the poor father is still alive [we will soon see that this is not the case] and that this is the only consolation that I can provide: to avenge his sweet and beautiful daughter who was arrested like one arrests a bandit, and who on the night of her arrest was forced to listen to the harshest words that anyone can ever hear. It was Chief B. who dared speak to her in this way. He, too, deserves to be punished, but he was simply doing as he was ordered. It is his boss who should be punished first.

The boss who only acted because he believed that the child had no one to protect her. The boss who tried to buy himself a good reputation at the end of his career by performing a couple of seemingly patriotic actions. But for this boss it was as if he were handing over an angel. I mean that literally, sir, because truly this girl was perfection. I am attaching a photo of her in order to convince you.

To the service of the innocent, I will dedicate my life. I hope that I will avenge the girl in Melle. If I fail, I will join forces with her father in Paris . . .

A Mere Transfer

It is an understatement to say that Madame Picard's deposition had no effect. After reading her letter the president of the purification committee in Melle informed the body in executive session that the matter of the "Jewess from Lié" had been taken care of by "a state police colonel charged with this task." His verdict handed down without argument amounted to an acquittal. "Don't go there!," as any cop might say to a driver at a traffic stop! Captain T. was transferred, following complaints about him, but the colonel who was responsible for the verdict had decreed that "it was not possible to consider filing a more serious complaint," even if it were proven that he was responsible for the arrest of the "Jewess from Lié."

To be more effective, Madame Picard decides to file a complaint herself. Since such a complaint was supposed to be supported by relatives of the injured party, she reaches out to Ida's uncle and aunt, the Dembskis, which the police in Clamart had done a better job of protecting than the brigade in Melle. Her letter is dated January 22, 1945, which is to say at the time when Ida was on "the death march" between Auschwitz and Ravensbrück. . . .

> Dear Friends,
>
> I am here to ask you to do me an enormous service: I have undertaken to seek justice for our little Ida, and to this end I have filed a complaint against Captain T., from Melle. After a short while I learned that he

> had been transferred to Nîmes, but still at the rank of captain, and this I will not accept. So I went to the liberation committee[59] in Niort and I was told that this would certainly be all the punishment he would get. I was given to understand that since it was not the family that was filing the complaint, it was a waste of time to take the deposition of a mere schoolteacher.
>
> After having gotten some information from a friend who went to Paris, here is the procedure we intend to follow, and to do this we must count on your goodness:
>
> You must file a complaint against Captain T., from Melle, for having taken away your niece in the middle of the night of January 30 to 31, 1944. . . . How happy her parents would be if they knew that we were joining in our efforts to avenge their child! . . . Let this be a secret between us. This is how to do it. . . .

Following this she gives a summary of the events, and advice on how to write the complaint, not failing to mention the mayor's effort to establish Ida's French nationality and the words of "Chief B." to Alice Marché: "Do you want to be shot yourself?" "Do you want us to shoot you?" or "You will never see her again."

The liberation committee in Paris acknowledged receipt of the complaints by calling for details—already supplied—on Captain T. and the nature of the orders given to him. In June of 1945, the committee in Melle expressed its view that the arrest was "extremely unfortunate" but "it does not follow from [its] description" that any error was committed by the police, which would itself have been confronted "by the impossibility of doing otherwise." The policeman B. appears to have "spoken very harshly" and demonstrated a "lack of tact" [*sic*], but T's transfer seemed to be "sufficient" and "should not harm his career," since he had acted "under the influence of fear" and not "out of pro-German sympathies."

Case closed!

The true, and rather petty, tale: one learns that Captain T., so quickly absolved of any crime, was not just acting out of fear of the occupying forces. The book that earned him an appearance on television in 1970, and his being recognized by Ida, was already being written by him during the war. It bears witness to his being of a like mind as the

Pétainist establishment, and leads one to believe that he endorsed the orders handed down in January 1944. In the preface to what is itself simply a collection of police reports all involving "psychic" phenomena, the author had received words of encouragement, general but distinctly warm, from Alexis Carrel, a biologist known for his eugenic theories and a member of the inner circle in Vichy.

As for Colonel D., who so diligently moved to clear his colleague T., his own record from the 1940s is blank! Which will not stop him from following a lofty career path, complete with a general's stars, and being assigned the most distinguished duties in the state police following the war.

It is common to ask for leniency in the face of such flexible standards, both in conscience and in hiring practices, on the grounds that chance plays a part, so that responsibility cannot be strictly assigned in political matters. The answer to such excuses can be found in the letter from Camus accompanying his signature of the petition to spare the life of Brasillach: "I do not know whether chance enters into political opinions or not. But I do know that it plays no part in choosing to dishonor yourself."[60]

"My Best Student"

The complaints filed against the police by Madame Picard in 1944 and 1945 reveal the strength of her attachment to Ida. Following her return, and with regularity, the former pupil bore witness to her grateful affection for her schoolteacher. Since the primary school teacher from Sompt was still alive when this book was being written, how could we not have gotten in touch to hear her tell the story in her own voice of a past in which she played a real part?

Our visit took place in September of 2001, on a glorious autumn day. The retirement home in Melle is called "Les Charmilles." The sun pours into Madame Picard's ground floor bedroom. The historian of the region, Jean-Marie Pouplain, accompanies us for this great leap back into memories that were then already sixty years old.

A smallish room, a television, some family photos, a wheelchair: the whole setup is modest, in keeping with a lifetime that knew of no other luxuries than those derived from the joy of teaching. Her face is marked by ninety years of wear. But you forget her age the moment she recalls the emotions of the school in Sompt, so named because of the river that crosses it, la Somptueuse. Her face, especially, lights up, smiling, teasing, incredibly rejuvenated when she sets eyes on her former pupil, thanks to whom she had experienced so much happiness and concern.

The former teacher wraps her arms around the one she still calls "her li'l Ida," in the rough accent of the countryside. Ah, her "li'l Ida!" This adjective, "little," has followed Ida through her entire life. The

Vichy establishment, eager to align itself with the German persecution, spoke of the "Jewess of Lié." In the heat of the moment, the liberation committee in Melle picked up the expression, as if the description hadn't been enough to send a person to her death only a day earlier. The word "Jewess" has disappeared—finally!—but in the village the adjective "little" remains, undoubtedly in recognition of the very young age at which Ida was deported, or because of her size, which remained small into adulthood. When she meets former friends from the camps, during her travels, the childhood diminutive sticks with her, and she is recognized as being one of the youngest to survive.

Madame Picard's gaze sharpens with mischief.

"She was one of my best students ever," she says. (She pauses, then corrects herself as she did when, as a teacher, she played at testing the impatience and the pride of the "top students.") "Okay, I guess I can say it now: she was *the* best!"

Then she nails her case shut with a final proof:

"She beat out the boys! The top! Even the agreement of past participles when using the verb *avoir*, just to give you an idea!"

Had she in fact allowed Ida to become the teacher's pet? Madame Picard protests:

"With me there were no favorites! That was not my style! Ida was number one, that's all there was to it."

A professional reflex: having remained a teacher to the very last, Madame Picard searches for the fairest judgement, worthy of being written on a student's report card:

"Ida was without pretention, entertaining, but without trying to be noticed. She used her wits to be like everyone else. While she was the 'little Parisian,' she quickly picked up the local way of speaking."

The former servant of the Republic—thirty-seven and a half years of teaching, she declares with pride—she recalls that in the early days she was expected to help stamp out local dialect, while today people are hired to teach it!

"The world is upside down!" she grumbles.

At school, no student ever made any remarks about Madame Picard's protegée. "Ida was from here, period, end of story."

When did Madame Picard start to worry for her pupil? To answer this question she reverts immediately to the passive voice and the carefully measured phrases of the academy:

"You are arrested when, little one?"

Ida also reverts to the earnest tone of the schoolgirl she once was:

"The night of the thirtieth of January, ma'am."

"So, the particular threats began six months prior."

In reality, the danger started when Ida was officially recognized as being "Jewish," which is to say in June of 1942, when the yellow stars were distributed.

The office of inspection of the School Board ("which obeyed the Germans' orders," Madame Picard points out, with names of civil servants on the tip of her tongue) sent an official form to the city hall asking the school if Ida was still in Sompt, and whether she had learned a trade. Madame Picard advised Alice Marché to not keep Ida at home with her in Lié.

"'Can you imagine? The Germans here? Surely they have other things to do!'"

"At least stop getting a food ration card in her name!" the teacher insisted.

Alice protested: "'Then what will she eat?'" She didn't want to hear any suggestion about Ida boarding as an apprentice under an assumed name at Chef Boutonne[61] either. Madame Picard loses patience over this:

"No, but really! Ida was not about to keep a flock of sheep for the rest of her life!"

The teacher has forgotten nothing. She remembers that Ida's mother was arrested in July 1942 and that she came regularly to Lié by bicycle to "buck up" her daughter's spirits. For an entire year Madame Picard kept Ida in her class while giving her extra tutoring in algebra and French.

Then came the arrest on January 30, 1944. Alice went to see Madame Picard in tears to tell her. She in turn told her inspector, who advised her to do nothing, or she would risk being sent to a concentration camp herself. Alas, yes: the employees of the state education department were not always more honorable than those in the police force!

Did she have any idea as to the fate that awaited her pupil?

"Heavens! I was sure that Ida was at risk for her very life! After the letter from her mother, there was no longer any possible doubt. (Silence) I blamed it on the captain of the state police more than anyone else, he who pretended to be the friend of our mayor, Monsieur Poupinot! It was he who had suggested that we stop claiming a ration card for Ida. He swore he would warn us if there were any threat. . . . We saw what that was worth!"

"Even Raymond!"

How did the class react to the news that Ida had been arrested? Madame Picard tells the story, as if it happened yesterday:

"I informed the children that their comrade Ida had been taken away by the French, on the orders of the Germans. I told them: 'Think of her always. Never forget. When you are falling asleep at night, think of her. Promise?' I was crying. I couldn't stop crying. My tears flowed all the way up to heaven . . ."

Madame Picard's indignation has not subsided over time. She raises her voice:

"Children! What wrong had they done, by Golly!"

She can see the class, stunned, before her:

"And Raymond! How he could cry, Raymond!"

Raymond was the little neighbor boy whom Ida helped in French and who helped her with arithmetic. They were in love with each other. It was her letters from Raymond that Ida took pains to destroy, the night when the police came to arrest her, for fear that Alice would scold her when she found out about their correspondence . . .

At this, Ida remembers the feelings they shared in Sompt, sixty years earlier. Raymond came to see her in the Broussac hospital when she returned from the camps. The spark that lit up their lives before all hell broke loose failed to reignite. No matter: Ida simply could not believe that Raymond had cried, on learning of her arrest.

In Madame Picard's room, this news from the distant past makes Ida feel slightly giddy. Little Ida lets out a burst of youthful joy that is still intact after all the trials she has been through. She shows a tender surprise, unaware of the vigor in her words, spoken softly "as if for herself alone":

"Really? Raymond cried? Even him?"

The Missed Meeting with Wanda

Ida was not as fortunate with her benefactor Wanda as she was with Madame Picard. Fate did not allow them to see each other again. But at least the missed appointment had other results, like the project to write this book.

Ida tried to identify Wanda repeatedly over more than fifty years in order to thank the woman for saving her life in the *Revier* at Neustadt.

In 1988, in the course of her first return trip to Auschwitz, in the confused state of her emotions at the time, she mentioned the name of the nurse over and over. She tried everything, including phoning during a television broadcast on the show "*Perdu de vue.*"[62] The producers would have loved to try this unusual procedure, but an assistant found that the technology at that time did not permit a "direct hookup with Poland"! Ida was not happy with this excuse. A call while on the air might have allowed her to make progress going back up the trail to Wanda before it was too late.

It was only in early 2001 that a German citizen in Neustadt, a Mr. Shutt, found Wanda's family name in a directory of former workers in the *Revier:* Ossowska. Armed with this information, the head of the guides at Auschwitz, Mr. Stanczyk, found Wanda in the lists for Auschwitz, where she had also been interned. She was still alive, living in Warsaw.

Contact is finally made. Ida is on the verge of departure for Poland. But Wanda doesn't want to be visited before she recovers from a stroke she has had. She writes to her "little daughter"—Ida definitely moves everyone to use the affectionate diminutive—a letter that she then has translated by her relatives. Some words of note:

> I thought of you very often, I even told your story in my book, which was published in Poland. What did you become? How did you make it through all of those terrible years after the end of the war?
>
> In the camps of Neustadt-Glewe you were my child, condemned to death, whom I wanted to save forever and for all. But what means did I have at my disposal? At that time, I found Love—the supernatural strength which allowed me to save you.
>
> I remember well: you shouted "Long Live France!" though you were unconscious. For you I saved that terrible soup that people back then waited for like it was chocolate from a gift package that never existed.
>
> When I dressed you up like a little old lady, the German tormentor, either he thought I was nuts or else he found in his heart a little bit of love—he let me save you.
>
> I remember well the French soldiers from the Oflag who picked you up from the hospital.[63] You were still unconscious and I sent you off with all the hope and the love in my heart.
>
> I begged the Lord insistently to save you, my little Ida! And you are alive, Ida!
>
> I am so happy to hear from you, and I hope to see you in Warsaw.
>
> Excuse me for calling you "Ida," but you remain forever my child.
>
> Right now, I am in the hospital, but I am confident that God will save me again.
>
> Hoping to hold you in my arms, I send you my best wishes for you and your family.
>
> Wanda Ossowska

Fate only allowed Ida to see her nurse again in a coma. She died without Ida's being able to tell her how grateful she was, except at her funeral—a burial service worthy of a true heroine, of a saint even, where Ida held a place of honor.

Exceptional Women

On the evening of November 1, 2001, at the end of a teachers' trip to Auschwitz and Majdanek,[64] Wanda Ossowska's grandnephews received us in the suburbs of Warsaw.

One of the relatives played the videocassette that he had made several years prior with his great-aunt telling her life to the youngest children in her family. Ida recognized the somber gaze, sparkling with intelligence, of the nurse in Neustadt, her hair in a tight bun, and especially her deep voice.

While we watch the family document, the grandniece who organized the evening and who is the only one who speaks any French, translates the passage from Wanda's book that describes rescuing Ida.

> "They bring a little French girl who is unconscious into the infirmary where I find myself.
>
> "'Can you save her?' they ask. There are no children in the camp. If the Germans see her, they'll shoot her.
>
> "The child is delirious. Her feet are black, frozen. I am afraid that necrosis has already begun. She was a very pretty girl. Her cheeks were red with fever. Her condition made me feel sick to my stomach. Could I save her? She has dysentery. Her sphincters have let go. She absolutely must have a bath. I am afraid she will lose her toes. One phalange has already separated.
>
> "I alternate hot and cold baths to stimulate circulation. They didn't tell me the child's name. I call her 'the Little One' and 'my child.' Her

toes became pink again. In her coma she shouted: '*Vive la France!*'"

Getting out of bed, the Little One fell down. They searched for her in the dark. There was excrement on the floor. They can't wash her off without turning on the light. I refuse to hand over the girl's sweater to the German woman who demanded it.

I learn that there is going to be a selection.[65] What should be done with the little French girl? I wrap a scarf around her head to hide the curls that are starting to grow back. I undress her. I pray. A tall soldier from the Gestapo comes in. He says, surprised:

"'But she is just a child!'

"I say 'no.'

"'You are an idiot,' says the soldier.

"It didn't matter. The child was spared.

"I don't know what became of her, if she survived or not. I kept saying to her: 'Eat, if you want to return home!'"

Wanda's book contains another staggering testimonial:

"A woman had a baby in the camp four months earlier. She succeeded in hiding the baby by having it sleep during the daytime. A soldier discovered the newborn. He took it by the feet and slammed it against the wall until it was dead.

"'I cannot live without my baby,' begged the mother. "'Shoot me!'"

"The soldier granted her wish with a burst from his pistol . . ."

Since the month of May 2001, when Ida saw Wanda again, alas, in a coma, she has not stopped feeling strong warmth coming from her family. They too have doubtless felt the same thing. When she came back for the nurse's funeral, she experienced feeling like she had become a very close part of the family.

"Following my visit in November 2001, this feeling only became stronger the time when I was shown the videocassette which they made a copy of for me to keep. To see Wanda speaking, alive, to recognize her voice, slightly older but having the same timbre, that moved me in an unbelievable way. One can sense how her feelings are backed up by her competence as a nurse, but also with fundamental intelligence. She was an impressive woman. I only learned about her experience in the resistance after her death. When I knew her I was only aware of her tremendous goodness and her skill at what she did."

Her own mother, Alice, Madame Picard, Wanda, her girlfriends in the camps, the resisters in Switzerland: Ida's greatest luck came from the collection of exceptional women whom she met and who helped her along the way!

"The Only Cemetery I Have"

From October 29 until November 2, 2001, we took part in a trip organized by the Association of Former Deportees of Auschwitz/Birkenau[66] to both Auschwitz and Majdanek, in the company of fifty faculty members and librarians. On the flight home, Ida reflected on the trip:

"Since the first time I went back, in March 1988, I have been back to the camps approximately twenty times, always with groups of schoolchildren, to answer their questions. I couldn't say anymore what emotions or thoughts predominated during each visit apart from the one obvious consistent, obsessive reaction, which is that Birkenau is the place that is hardest to really grasp.

"Auschwitz is first of all a museum. The first time I almost fainted, in the big hall where one can see an enormous pile of hair. I realized that my mother's hair must be in there. If she made it into the camp or not they shaved her head. I had the same reaction in front of the pile of personal effects. The feeling is less strong now than it was the first time, but it comes back each time that I see the arrival ramp at Birkenau.

"Not because of my recalling 'selection,' because I really didn't know what was happening; but to find oneself there, exhausted, in the snow, with the SS who were all shouting orders every which way. It is much more powerful for me than Majdanek, where the monument is very moving, but whose barracks and bunks don't remind me of anything. In Birkenau I see myself going to work and coming back, living in the blocks.

"Especially I have the sensation that I am approaching the burial site of my parents. When you walk towards the lake, if you just scratch the ground a bit, you know that you are going to come to ashes. It is the only cemetery that I have where I can express my feelings. It is the biggest cemetery in the world, a record number of dead per square yard. There is none other like it. I come in order to be useful, but also out of piousness. I have no other gravesite where I can pay my respects, I have only this place. I don't interpret the fact that wind blows our candles out as a symbol of how difficult it is to reach the departed. We just need to bring lamps with better wind protection like they have in the cemeteries in Warsaw, which last for at least a day."

To the university people present, Ida explained how she and her friends organized a round-robin with the blanket that was too thin and too narrow to keep the whole bunk warm. This gesture of solidarity was the way of gaining back an appearance of freedom, a little bit of the humanity that the guards had confiscated. Remember that for lack of enough room, they all had to go to sleep on the same side, and all turn over at the same time, on cue. That builds a bond between people.

"Were you bothered by the smell of your neighbors?"

"We all smelled, given the lack of hygiene, the dysentery! We all realized it ourselves, it was demoralizing. We were put off by our own smell. We noticed snoring less. We were so tired that we fell into deep sleep the moment we collapsed on our straw mattress."

"Did you dream?"

"We dreamed of many things. Especially about food. We dreamed that we were escaping, that we were free. We imagined our lives following the camp. Waking up was even harder because of this, when the *kapo* started yelling at us, before dawn, at four in the morning."

Only as Long as a Song

A supposition in the form of a wish comes to mind: towards the end, when Germany was going to lose the war, didn't it happen that an old guard or a *kapo* found compassion for you, revealed herself to be less severe, more understanding, if only to be able to claim this good deed at the hour of reckoning, which was drawing closer?

Ida has no doubts:

"It was impossible! In Ravensbrück I didn't work; in Neustadt I was in the *Revier.* I never experienced any such reversal. But in truth I must say that some of my comrades did.

"It happened to Rosette, for one. She had a serious accident at the Union Werke factory, on a machine that had no protective shield. She had two phalanges on one of her fingers cut off. An overseer accompanied her to the *Revier* to be treated. On the way there, Rosette made a point of honor of not showing the woman how much pain she was in. She, too, 'did not cry.' She started to sing, in order to keep her spirits up. The German looked at her, astonished.

"Nazi propaganda had convinced her that a Jewess was incapable of courage. She started singing the same song as Rosette, only in German. Their exchange was limited to this one moment of shared singing. Our comrade spent a long time in the *Revier* because of recurring infections. When she returned to the factory, the same overseer recognized her and, without saying a word, she found the girl less strenuous assignments."

In the movies, the refrain taken up in unison by the executioner and the victim might be *Lily Marlene*,[67] the famous wartime song sung by soldiers on both sides in the conflict.

Thus, thanks to Rosette's nerve, humanity and brotherhood recovered their rightful place, although without admitting to it entirely, in Auschwitz. This was a rare and unspoken exception to the rule, and for the briefest of moments. As Serge Gainsbourg famously sang in *La Javanaise:* it only lasted as long as a song.[68]

The Thoughts of a Witness

What impression does Ida retain from her many trips to the camps with school groups?

Both similar and varied, at the same time. Ida explains what she means by this:

"The participants and their questions resemble each other. I have a very striking impression of one group I was with last year, more motivated than usual. That doesn't mean that others were less interested. Seniors are obviously better informed, prepared.

"The Association of Former Deportees of Auschwitz/Birkenau is aware that teachers will be more useful, quantitatively, in the transmission of information than the pupils; thirty or forty times as much. They know through experience that the teachers who have visited the camps are no longer the same and their teaching is strengthened by it. History textbooks become improved. It is the number of hours spent on the subject that is insufficient.

"Travel to the sites deeply transforms the participants. They speak about the experience willingly. As with this librarian from around La Rochelle,[69] who writes her impressions spontaneously:"

> Wednesday, October 29, 2001, Auschwitz.
>
> Dear Ida, just a few words to tell you how much I thank you for all that we are learning right now. About what you are. Not only did the Nazis not destroy you physically, they did not touch your deep humanity

which is manifest everywhere, in your intelligence to transmit your experience, your vivacity, your energy, your sense of human relationships, your taste for life, your laicity,[70] and your refusal to pass moral judgment, which I appreciate above all, because behind it there is a deeper moral that I love. I send you loving kisses.

PART III

Then What?

When you returned in 1945, how would you describe your energy level and your "will to live?" Ida jumps right into it:

"To have children. Rebuild a family! My dream was always to have three children. I got married in 1953. My daughter Sophie was born after we were married eight years; I was giving up hope. I went into a deep depression following the delivery. Because I didn't have my mother, it took on horrendous proportions. I couldn't sleep, I lost my appetite. So my husband decided that we weren't going to try that again. It is the greatest regret in my life. One child is not enough. You have to have at least two."

Why 1988?

There is still a mystery surrounding the history of the memory, both individual and collective, of these events. How can one explain the relative silence of survivors from 1945 until well into the 1980s: forty-three years in Ida's case, from her return to the Hôpital Broussais to her first pilgrimage back to Auschwitz in 1988.

Ida adopts the explanation of historians. First one, then two, generations passed. Curiosity sprang back to life, interest sharpened. Books and films caused or simply accompanied a renewal of interest in the Shoah. Holocaust denial had taken what advantage it could of the brief eclipse. Did it work?

"And how! To see people deny what we had lived through was unbearable. It amounted to killing our comrades who had disappeared all over again! We discussed this in our association meetings. People were saying things we simply could not put up with.

"It was the lawyer and historian Serge Klarsfeld who convinced me to take part in a trip scheduled for March of 1988, which was being organized by the World Jewish Congress and the CRIF.[1] For me, it would be the first time I returned to the camp after forty-three years! He called me on a Sunday for departure on the following Wednesday. I wasn't sure that I would be able to go. He found an argument that clinched it: it was going to be the first trip when they took young people, and the pupils were all just a little older than I was at the time I was there; it would be useful to have me along! On Monday, I would apply for a visa at the Polish consulate. In fact, I was terribly shaken."

The word "shaken" is mild. It was during this trip that we met for the first time, Ida and Bertrand, and that our friendship began. Ida was stumbling between the ruins of barracks, trying to find her own. The ground was frozen, the sky was low. The young people hesitated to ask questions. For Ida, the place was above all a cemetery, the burial place of her parents. You don't talk a lot standing around a grave. Night fell early. It wasn't yet about describing the site and what had happened there, it was about demystifying the place, stepping into it in order to make talking about it possible at last.

Which is not to say that one gets used to it. At the rate of from one to two visits a year there, Ida must have visited it twenty times. She has never gotten comfortable with it. Each time it is a painful challenge to be overcome. The formal History is intertwined with a history of memory, with its dark shadows and inexplicable "transformations." Transformations don't necessarily mean "deformations": in the six months spent editing this book, interviews were gone over again and again, compared, rewritten. Bertrand can attest that Ida did not change her story by one iota. She watched over and weighed every word as if it were a book about someone else, as if she was now watching over "little Ida" herself.

What Is It to Bear Witness?

The "willing silence" of the survivors is legendary, and it has been kept current as an excuse for not talking about all of this by disinterested audiences in the postwar era. Ida is certain as to her own attitude:

"Starting immediately after my return, I felt the need to tell. I answered every time people asked me about it. If I didn't speak at length it was because people didn't want to listen for very long. It began right away in the hospital. In Switzerland, we were all ex-detainees with nothing to teach each other. But I was learning about the Resistance, from women who had been in it and who had suffered because of that. I envied them because they had been able to fight, to have survived out of idealism, while I had been arrested for nothing but the fact that I was Jewish. For their part, they were learning about the attempt to exterminate us. In their eyes, I was "the baby" of the rehabilitation center. They showed me a great deal of kindness.

"Right away in Montana I met Geneviève de Gaulle. She was at the hotel, not far from our villa. She came to see us regularly. Her being related to the general didn't matter much to us. She never mentioned it. Somewhat after the fact I came to admire the undertaking that was Free France.[2] I wore a Cross of Lorraine with pride on a little chain. In those days we were not asking ourselves the questions that would come up later, like the reasons why the Allies did not bomb or intercept the convoys, since they 'knew' about the horror of the camps.

"Geneviève had problems with her voice. Despite that fact she gave talks on the role of women in the Resistance to finance rest homes that she sponsored. We accompanied her, seated on stage around her. One day the attendees gave her a bouquet of flowers which she turned and gave to me! I felt it was important that this book include as an epigraph a sentence by her that sums up so well the lesson of solidarity brought back from the camps.

"In Switzerland I also met Charlotte Delbo, who was already working on her book *None of Us Will Return* that she didn't want to publish until twenty years later, in 1965, since she felt that before that the French people 'weren't ready to accept it.'

"When I returned to the Deux-Sèvres region, following Switzerland, people asked me questions. In my work as a seamstress, too. But people have their own problems. They are not ready to listen. Moreover, in these workshops, many of the employees were Jewish, and they had friends and relatives who had disappeared. They really did not want to hear what suffering the deportees had gone through. This led me to be somewhat reticent. But I always answered. I am not one of those who remained silent by choice.

"I had nothing to teach my husband: his mother had been deported two weeks before mine, when he was fourteen. He told me how he was hidden. We shared the experience of motherlessness.

"It was around 1960–1970 that books and films began to change people's awareness of the Shoah. I saw them, I read them, when they came out. *Shoah*, the film by Claude Lanzmann, is a benchmark monument. *Night and Fog* didn't tell me anything I didn't know. I remember *The Last Stage*, photographs of piles of dead bodies, were more evocative of camps like Bergen-Belsen.[3] Personally, I didn't see these things. Auschwitz was better 'organized'; they burned the bodies there as they went along. In one sense what we saw was even worse. It was less the dead bodies, and more about walking skeletons, zombies.

"The students whom I meet want to know how people arrived at the final stage. When I speak to them, I focus on the progression of stages of exhaustion: hunger that causes sharp stomach pains; the cold, the filth, the beatings. The mutilated bodies of prisoners seen at the liberation of the camps were the result of slow, painful torture. Films will never trace this progression. It was sometimes less affecting to see dead bodies than to see the standing dead, too weak to walk.

"As far as books are concerned, the one that made the strongest impression on me was *None of Us Will Return*, by Charlotte Delbo. I must say, in all modesty and not at all as a literary critic, that Primo Levi always struck me as extremely pessimistic."[4]

And what are conversations about between former detainees themselves?

"The Friendship Society was founded in 1945. I joined very early. I didn't go as often as I would have liked, because I lived on the other side of Paris. I had the good fortune to be part of a small group made up of women who had known each other in the camp. The Friendship Society created '*rencontre*' (meeting) very early on, which was an annual gathering on the last Sunday of January, the anniversary of the liberation of Auschwitz. We always made great discoveries at these meetings.

"The camp didn't make some social distinctions go away. Claudine, for one, was from a more privileged milieu. I didn't have the means to have a new dress made for myself in order to attend her wedding. I also found Liliane Badour[5] again thanks to '*rencontre*.'"

"Who Did That to You?"

How did she tell the story to her family?

"My daughter Sophie began asking me questions before she was even five years old. It was my identification number tattooed on my arm that intrigued her. She didn't think it was 'pretty.' She asked me:

"What's that? Who did that to you?"

"Some people who were not nice, bad people."

Sophie frowned:

"Well, you will tell me who it was that did that. And me, I am going to do the same thing to them."

Fortunately, she grew up free of hatred, but that was her reflex response to the tattoo. She added:

"Did it hurt?"

"Not really. It stung a bit at first, but it didn't really hurt."

For her, what was clear is that I was not like everybody else. Afterwards, she started asking questions about her grandparents.

"Why don't I have any grandmothers?"

"They died during the war. And it was the same bad people as the numbers who killed them."

I didn't mention that they were Germans. It was "bad" people, that was all. When she was seven or eight, Sophie came across some photographs in a shoe box. She asked who was "the little girl with no hair," the ID photo taken when I returned from the camps. She didn't want to believe it was me. And once she learned this, she didn't want to look at the pictures again. She was afraid. She wanted to be sure that she wouldn't see "the little girl." Following that, she learned a lot of things by listening to my conversations with my former girlfriends. Since then she has also watched cassettes of my meetings with schoolchildren. What she knows, she learned like that."

Up until when she became an activist in the telling of her own story, did Ida harbor any ill feeling towards the "bad" people? Had she found that she detested the German language, as did the philosopher Jankelevitch?[6]

"I can understand his decision on principles. It is true that I had a negative memory of the language in which we were tortured. I have only returned to Germany for trials, the one with Lischka and Hagen, for example.[7] I was in Cologne to demonstrate against a delay in the proceedings. It would never occur to me to go to Germany or Austria as a tourist."

What impact did the trials in Nuremberg or the trial of Eichmann[8] have on her?

"During the Nuremberg trials, I was in Switzerland. There were no portable transistor radios then. We didn't listen. When I got back, I thought that they had tried very few Nazis, and had talked very little about the Shoah. In 1961 I followed the Eichmann trial in the newspapers. While I was against the death penalty, I did not think that Eichmann deserved to live. I hold less against the Nazis for what they did to me than for what they did to my parents. I would prefer to have seen the woman who turned my father in tried rather than the policemen in Melle! It is an entire machine that needs to be condemned, but the individual people involved! I did not go to Lyon for Barbie's trial,[9] one needed authorizations that I did not have. I attended two sessions in the trial of Touvier.[10] I was sick at the time Papon was being tried."[11]

There is one area yet to be explored: Between 1945 and 1988, when you made your first trip back to the scene, what happened to memory itself? How did it change?

"At first, I was not actively speaking out because nobody was asking me to. Schools were not seeking witnesses to come and speak. Once again, it was the argument of 'usefulness' that governed where I went.

Guides at that time spouted their information as if their audience was made up of ordinary tourists. The immediacy of our accounts changed how they did things."

Were the questions from the pupils all similar? What did they ask you?

"Many questions come back again and again. What is remarkable is that the students are really shaken at the end of my account. The teachers have prepared the classes, more or less. The work of the Lycée Buffon in Paris, which won the Prix Corrin in 2001 for its efforts, is a model of this kind of thing.[12] It is not enough to be exact and precise. An example: in 1988, M. P. was doing useful work as a guide to Auschwitz. But then he found some documents about the delivery of the ovens from the manufacturer; and at that same time we learned that he had begun to favor the views of some Holocaust deniers, and he was letting this creep into his remarks to the students. Can this kind of thing be cured?

"There is one sight that floors me still, each time I visit the camp: it is the mountain of human hair. I don't think about my own shaven head. I think about my mother's hair. Since the Germans constantly repurposed it, hers must have been used for something. But I keep thinking that maybe there are locks of my mother's hair in that pile along with all the rest! When they shaved us, this is what struck me, the long locks of hair lying like braids on the floor. I never found out where the girls who shaved us came from.

"All of the tours with school kids happen in more or less the same way. I introduce myself to the students in a few words. In less than an hour, I have told about how I was living in the countryside, about the arrest and what Alice did to try and get me out, the week spent in Drancy, the train trip and the first day in Auschwitz. Then we talk. Many of them ask me my opinion of *Schindler's List,* which I think was very well made, but it doesn't have much to do with Auschwitz, which can't be filmed, really. *Holocaust* was very romanticized, but the series helped build awareness in Germany and in America. In the same way, I do not wish to criticize Benigni's film, as long as it is understood that the movie is not about the deportation.[13] I already said that Lanzmann's

Shoah is a monumental piece. The broadcasts of trials are also useful. It is too bad that Bousquet was never put on trial."[14]

Lessons for today?

"I acknowledge in front of the students that, of course, we felt hatred for the guards and the *kapos*. After the war, when I ran into Germans of a certain age group, tourists, I wondered what they did during the war. But after almost sixty years, one can no longer call this hatred. The danger is Nazism, and that exists in strength as much in France and in Belgium as it does in Germany and Austria.

"I have spoken to groups of young people from Germany. For me, they are simply Europeans. That being said, they do show some obvious discomfort. I did this through the *Centre de Documentation juive contemporaine* (Center for Contemporary Jewish Documentation) in Paris. It was a class of German high school seniors, and they came accompanied by their French teacher.

"They are a part of the third generation. They are in no way guilty on account of what happened, even if some of their relatives were closely connected to Nazism. When I speak to them about this, I feel a sense of relief. Some of them say that in their homes this subject never comes up. Others confirm that it is something they have considered discussing but haven't yet. They do not talk about the responsibility of their country as if it were a thing of the past."

Good Questions

Ida keeps a record of her meetings with student groups. It's a green notebook, the color of hope. After having begun to bear witness in order to be useful——and not as a form of therapy, as one student suggested—she has gone through her conversations with people a generation or two younger than she to find what she thinks are some good reasons not to worry about the future.

The questions are sometimes naive, but most are "good questions." They are the ones that led the former detainee at Auschwitz to recognize what really mattered at the time, and what continues to matter. When their teachers hadn't filled in all the blanks, it was simply a matter of explaining what the *kommandos* or the *kapos* really were. One by one the reasons for surviving were teased out and underscored in response to the kids' questions. Ida recounts each one with intense feeling: the fact that she understands German (via Yiddish); the camaraderie among the students . . .

The most frequent questions?

"Did you ever think about escaping?" (The frequency of this question can be explained by the fact that children are themselves impatient, and to move the experience of the camp along as we are all in a hurry to leave. Very soon, for the same reasons, they want me to talk about my liberation.) The answer: "It was impossible to escape, given the rows of barbed wire, the watch towers, our shaved heads, the striped rags that we were wearing, the complete lack of friends on the outside, our lack of knowledge of the language spoken in the area, Polish. Girls tried, they quickly realized that it would be suicide to go through with it. We know, of course, that some deportees threw themselves on the electrified wires in order to 'be done with it.' As far as successful escapes go, I know only of the case of Mala. If you tried and failed—on the men's side, primarily—it was the noose, every time."

Another curiosity: "Was there solidarity, or was it everyone for herself, as some accounts would have it?"

"As far as I saw, solidarity had the upper hand. Not on the material level, since there was nothing to share, but in the physical and the moral sense. I benefited from this solidarity while on my way returning from work, and during the 'death march,' when I could no longer stand on my two feet."

Frequently heard: "Do you still feel hatred for the Germans?" "What do you think about how the guards behaved?" "When you returned, did you think about revenge?" "I answer that the desire to live an ordinary life like everyone else far outweighed any other. My goal was to manage to live without my parents, rather than to get even.

"Nuremberg? In Switzerland we were pretty much unaware of it. Were the trials of Touvier and Papon good? The answer is yes, they helped people to learn about the role of Vichy. The sentences passed matter less than the teaching value."

Do you still believe in God, after Auschwitz?

"I answer as I have said earlier: when one did not have faith going in, as was my case, the camp was no place to lose or to gain it! Did I ever experience moments of profound discouragement? Of course! But more often than not a tiny flame of confidence remained, a voice deep inside saying: 'We're going to get out of this place.' Without that hope, we would have sunk, never to return. One of the greatest challenges was to be patient once the landings in Normandy had happened: eleven months!

"When I am asked: 'How do you put up with injustice in the world today, as for example world hunger?' I answer that it is one of the hardest things for me to understand, how with all of the resources on this planet there can still be such misery. When you have suffered real pangs from hunger, you really understand what the people who are starving feel like.

“About my commitment to being a witness, I tell them that it is incorrect to say that when we returned from the camps we didn’t want to talk about it: it was really that people got tired of hearing about it very quickly. It is only in the past ten years that schools have really wanted it.[15] Three-quarters of the survivors alive today would be unable to make the trip back to Auschwitz, and I can understand that. Holocaust denial also played a part in my decision. It seemed to me that it was killing our parents a second time!

“One question that I really like: ‘Under what circumstances do you believe in disobedience?’ In fact there are orders that we have higher reasons to not follow. Naive curiosity: ‘Did you get mail?’ For ‘racial’ deportees, obviously not. No books, no paper, no pencils. Which did not prevent us from getting a little mental exercise. We told each other what happened in our favorite films. Some girls recited French poetry. We recalled verses by Victor Hugo on the retreat from Russia (Madame Picard had made us work hard on Hugo’s writings from exile): ‘It was snowing so hard. . . .’[16] I remember composing a poem for my friend Fanny who was arrested in the street because she hadn’t sewn the yellow star on, she had just pinned it (to be condemned to death for that!). Alas, I have forgotten that poem, and I couldn’t reconstitute it if I had to.

“Another more recent question: ‘Is it difficult to bear witness, or does it relieve you in some way?’ I have said it over and over again: No therapeutic benefit whatsoever! It’s a duty; a promise that I made to myself.”

The Need for Optimism

"For the most part, the students are sensitive to the difficulties that I encountered taking up my studies again after 'missing' so much school. A primary school certificate, far from a high school diploma: I was unclassifiable, unplaceable.

"One senses in children a need for optimism, a wish to hear that the guards at the camp had not lost their reflexes as human beings, that some of them even had performed 'good deeds,' in secret, or maybe towards the end, thinking that they were going to have to give some account of themselves. Some of my comrades have told stories like that. Personally it never happened to me. There was just the civilian employee at the factory who assigned the shortest girls to the assembly table, which was easier to reach than the other work stations; and the story of Rosette.

"The relative comforts of the guards still astonish me. Example: the bathtub of the superintendant of the ovens in Majdanek. To relax in the bath while the crematorium is working on the other side of the door, just like listening to jokes on the radio: how one can be so insensitive is a mystery to me! This was only possible because we had already been proclaimed to be 'subhuman' and were to be treated as such.

"The groups in which there were young people of color show a special concern: 'Do you think this could happen again?' I have absolutely no doubt: not in exactly the same way, but at the present time people are still being persecuted for nothing but where they come from! No talk about the Gulags, nor do I make comparisons with other genocides.[17] I don't contest the 'specificity' of the Shoah.

"I have heard people ask: 'Do you ever regret your Jewish origins?' which of course means: 'Without these origins you would not have been deported.' The obvious answer: I was born, that's all there is to it.

"The wackiest questions, which sometimes were painful because of the deep ignorance they reveal: 'Did you ever get to go on leave?' or worse: 'Who took care of your babies?' Faced with such a lack of understanding, one feels seized by dizziness, seriously depressed over where this is leading. Just to think that this kind of aberrant thinking might characterize majority thinking: what a nightmare!

"The saddest thing for us, the survivors, is that Auschwitz and its millions of dead might fail to serve as a lesson, a vaccine for humanity's ills. We absolutely believed that after the Shoah, genocide would no longer be possible, or even be tried. Wrong!"

"Salvation through Solidarity"

"Nobody would have survived if the Germans had thought to separate those detainees who, like our little group, shared the same language. Doubtless they couldn't even have conceived of it. To do that, they would have to have believed that we were capable of brotherhood, which would require having some respect for us. They were victims of their own contempt, on this point, and of their obsession with productivity. The solidarity that immediately united a handful of girls of the same age and speaking the same language has grown over time.

"This solidarity saved us, physically and in spirit. During the forced marches, we propped up the ones among us who were in danger of falling from starvation, always discreetly, in order to avoid their being selected. I mentioned telling film plots, during the *kommandos* at the factory, how we shared the single blanket. As soon as a buddy began to slip into depression, the group came together to bring her spirits back up. I don't know which was the more comforting, to be taken under the wing of a *koya*-mate or to be the one giving the help. Probably both.

"The recollections we share from the camp vary enormously depending on our own personalities. I learned this when I met Charlotte Delbo, during my convalescence in Switzerland. A member of the Young Communists in 1936, wife of a militant, arrested with him for acts of resistance in March 1942, deported to Auschwitz in January 1943, while her husband had been killed by a firing squad at the prison of Mont-Valérien the previous month of May. She wrote *None of Us Will Return,*

The Measure of our Days, and *Days and Memory.* I often reread her books. But I did not experience the same things as she. We had become friends. I drew this difference to her attention. Her conclusion was, and I believe this, that our moral suffering depended on how old we were.

"Her being nine years older was a disservice to her, even if her militancy helped her. My being fourteen and my lack of a shared past preserved me from having a more bitter awareness of the horror. My young age allowed me to remain in a permanent state of disbelief that helped me not to sink. To leave behind the start of a real life and people to miss weighs more heavily on a person than having one's entire future intact—or in any case the hope of having one."

Have I Forgotten Anything?

"At the moment of closing what will have been my last session as a witness—and the tragic nature of this 'last session' haunts me—I think about what I have left out, about how skimpy some of my remarks have been.

"For example, I am aware that I have not said a lot about the humiliations that we suffered, doubtless in part because I don't want to appear to be feeling sorry for myself, which is not my thing. But the latrines, hang on! You have to imagine a block of cement with dozens of round holes in alternating rows stretching on forever. We are led there in groups, on a set schedule. If you find you need to go in between times, and diarrhea is everywhere, fend for yourself! The filth and the odors, all of our memories are deeply imprinted by these to this day.

"Another thing the SS didn't foresee was the powerful inverse effect that their techniques of humiliation would have. The effort it took to stand up to the beatings and the insults ended up strengthening us, and brought us together. Here as well, the Nazi system suffered from its own excessive contempt for its victims. Geneviève de Gaulle said it quite well: 'Our way of resisting was to remain dignified, to remain human beings.'

"Another lesson: whatever the instinct for self-preservation might be, it is not equally instilled in us at birth, and one can only survive through the will to live. There is no getting around it. In this, my days spent in the countryside hardened me and made me more self-reliant. If only by the fact of having kept a flock of sheep!

"One day, for example, I was unable to keep a prowling dog from biting one of my sheep. Alice blamed me for the accident. The way she saw it, I was good for reform school. She fed me well, but she did not coddle me. She treated me like an adult, she was demanding. I fashioned dressings for the animal. We managed to save her. She gave birth to baby lambs. I derived a sense of victory from healing her. A laughable episode perhaps, but it definitely helped me grow.

"Other questions from students, summarized: Did I know of the existence of Hitler? I have already said that I had heard him on the radio (we called it the 'wireless' back then!) at the home of some friends of my parents. Before the war broke out, we knew that the Jews in Germany were being persecuted. Refugees told us about it, without any mention of the camps of course, although some of these, such as Dachau, had already opened. Basically, it was our absolute confidence in France, its hospitality and its military capability, which betrayed us. Even under Pétain, the Jews started out thinking that they would be protected. Some kinds of trust take a long time to dislodge! I take away one absolute conviction from all of this: to be betrayed by Vichy is not being betrayed by France.

"The proof is that many French people helped and hid Jewish families, especially children, often putting their own lives at risk in doing so. I want to recognize them for it and assure them of our eternal gratitude. They preserved the honor of France.

"I have already said my piece about religion. I didn't have it; so deportation did not threaten that. I mentioned that it did happen, when I was in the camp, that I trusted in Alice's faith. I was deeply touched that she insisted upon placing a statuette of the Virgin and an ex-voto plaque inscribed 'Thank you, 1945' in the little church in Sompt, where I pay my respects each time I visit the Poitou region. This acknowledgement having been made, I must state that the only higher values to which I subscribe, as did my father, are those of the secular republic. Those are the same ones taught by Madame Picard."

A Stone on the Edge of a Grave

"It sometimes happens that schoolchildren stare at the tattoo on my arm, without daring to exactly, a bit uncomfortable. Some have even asked me how it feels to wake up with these little blue numbers under my skin. It's simple: I think that one never really comes back completely from Auschwitz. I left a part of myself there, 'little Ida.' And my parents: my mother, who I knew had little chance of being alive very quickly once I arrived in the camp and I saw the state prisoners from 1942 were in; and my father, betrayed, gone in the last transport from France on July 31, 1944, whom I hoped for a very long time to see come home and will never know how and when he was murdered.

"What did the camps make me most sensitive to, and the most durably? To racism, in all its forms. We are all born with equal rights. The danger of totalitarianism is never headed off with any certainty. On a more physical level: I cannot stand to see anyone deprived of his freedom, or starve. This awakens pain in me that is still there after sixty years."

And the "duty to remember" that we do see challenged, judged useless, tiring, dangerous?

"I have said frequently that it is this duty that has led me to be a witness, to endure revisiting the camps. I know that my voice will be stilled soon. This book aims to project my words into the future. It will be the bouquet of flowers that we leave at the end of each of our visits, on the pond where ashes from the crematorium sank.

"It will be like the pebble that Jews leave on the edge of graves."

Do Not Ever Stop Telling

Just a little PS from Bertrand.

People often ask me what it is that connects me personally with the Shoah, coming from the outside, since I am not Jewish. This question has come from both inside and outside of the Jewish community, as often as not going very close to asking point-blank: "What right do you have?" One cannot deny that the question is worth asking.

I began to explain myself in our joint introduction. It is now or never to take that a step further.

A personal event happened that supported my first motivations: one of my daughters became the wife of a doctor whose ancestors were martyred, leaving him with doubts about France's hospitality, struggling as it was to recover from its racist wanderings during the war. Three of my grandchildren bear a name that would have put them at risk, sixty years ago. It happens that I imagine them with horror being among the persecuted in my own lifetime. My solidarity went from being a reasoned interest to a visceral concern. If aggravated, it could get out of control.

Not to disappoint the extremist rags that wished to see in my allegiance the beginnings of a philo-Semitic reaction, my signing up as an adopted Jew—I would like to say: honorary, if it were up to me—dates from my own childhood. I will say it again: French participation in the "Final Solution" seemed to me at the time, and has remained for me a scandal, a shame; an enigma, too. Beyond the memory of my classmate Riskine, I also preserve one from the nights in the spring of 1945 when

I helped greet the returnees brought over from the Gare de l'Est to the Hotel Lutétia.[18] I recall well how little the children weighed, who had to be carried; the feeling of dead wood, on our forearms, of their leg bones with no flesh on them at all; the smell of empty stomachs, of suffering, cold sweats, death throes, that had soaked into their ragged clothing.

Without these upheavals, plus my experience as a crime reporter in my early years in newspaper work, I would not have been drawn to cover all three of the trials for crimes against humanity, in 1987 (Barbie), 1994 (Touvier), and 1998 (Papon). I wrote articles and books about the first and the third of these. The Touvier trial helped me when I took part in Alain Ferrari's film on the Militia.[19] In and of itself the Touvier case didn't merit lingering over, except to throw light on the complicity of the Catholic Church in his flight from justice, and the poorly disguised persistence of his anti-Semitism. His defense team made exceptional use of a tactic that poses a broad threat to memory: to contradict the view of the majority of historians with the sole testimony of the accused, on the grounds that he knows better precisely because he is the only one to hold his opinion.

The Papon defense team picked up on this false symmetry and, arguing that the trial came long after the event, on recent attacks on the absence of statutes of limitations on crimes against humanity. Campaigns were mounted to interfere with, then to halt altogether the proceedings, or to represent them, with little credibility, as an anti-Gaullist plot, in the hope of bolstering the feebly asserted resistance record of this former Vichyite prefect.

People in favor of turning the page on the Dark Years (that's the accepted term, based on how they resemble each other) are not only to be found among former supporters of Vichy. Their motives are varied. Some are unfortunately well known: to deny or to minimize the crimes committed by the German and the French in the name of national and European reconciliation. Others, more respectable, are opposed to the Non-Applicability of Statutory Limitations to War Crimes and Crimes Against Humanity, including their application in cases involving the former Yugoslavia by the High Court in The Hague.[20] In doing so, in my opinion, they are mistaken, and we owe this advance in law and morality that faces down dictators and crimes of state everywhere to the legal response to Nazi barbarity.

Alongside the criticisms leveled at memory of the Shoah, we must not forget to save space for a word about historians who are obsessed with the disproportion, in their eyes, between the attention given to weighing the crimes of Hitler versus those of Stalin.[21] Through their insistent demand for a "Nuremberg for Communism," out of fear that the Soviet Gulags will go unpunished, they have come to believe that some of their detractors are biased in favor of the Soviets, as so many of them were themselves, and hopelessly in the grip of the lobby of Jewish survivors. This would be to forget that the Russian victims never called for such a purification, and that the Soviet Union, in its attempt to stamp out opposition, never aimed to wipe out an entire population, as was the case in the "Final Solution." This prolonging of the Cold War[22] in the historical community does not help anyone to draw reasoned conclusions from the madness of the twentieth century.

Generally speaking, it is fashionable to consider the testimony of the last witnesses as outworn long before they are dead, to denigrate all manner of attention and commemoration, and to rely only on the historical record. Everyone is free to read and reflect on the evolution of this history that is actually getting away from us now, philosophers like Ricoeur, historians like Rousso, Rémond, Azéma, Vidal-Naquet, and Jeanneney.[23] And make of them what they will! The conclusion of a book of testimonial is not the place to open a complex and personal debate on memory and what it imposes on us.

The why and wherefore of my involvement remains, and it refuses to go away under the pretext that reason was clearly understood. I maintain that the moment to shout out has not passed, indeed that it should never pass. In Greek and in Hebrew, *Zakkor* means both "you will remember" and "you will not stop telling." What would remain of Holy Scripture if it had not been repeated over and over again since the dawn of time, out of duty to repeat it over and over again? Almost no one sees the need to remember these things any more, in particular outside of the Jewish community. That's just one more reason not to let go.

Remarkably enough, for a member of my generation, in these past fifty years I never subscribed to any catechism or enlisted in any group that I need to renege on or regret. I have been an active militant against colonial wars, terrorism, and the growing inequality created by profit, but always without a label, except that of my newspaper. The obligations to find out the truth and to save lives seemed to me to take priority over partisan causes. I never signed any petitions on the grounds that people such as I who have access to public expression should not reinforce their opinions by such means of argument.

Memory of the Shoah, always under threat, appeared to me to be one of the rare causes worthy of being helped, because it is free of ulterior political motives and it needs militants. I read that, on this occasion, I was revealing my inner goy scout. I accept this teasing. For the same reasons I endorsed with relief the apologies of some Catholic bishops, because some sins of the Church under the Occupation had been committed in my name as one of the baptized.

My education has convinced me that individual and ethical commitment does not deserve the sneering doubts that it often attracts, including from me; it deserves them less than ideological zealotry in any case. Many different actions have grounded me in what I do not blush to call this attitude—and I mean just this: attitude, which is the opposite of a pose. Thus, quite apart from the Hotel Lutétia and the three trials, one can understand my involvement in varied works of memory and the many articles whose stridency I acknowledge. Thus one should also understand my relationship with Ida since 1988, and the task that is approaching completion here. For once the lining up of words, which was my profession and my passion, will perhaps serve something other than just pleasing me (which, let us agree, is not unimportant).

In closing, I want to remind the reader specifically of those memories of Ida that astonished me most and which justify, in my view, helping her testimony to stand against time: the rescuing of an injured sheep out of an obstinate love of life that was destined to save her life as well; her decision to give herself up (because she had a choice) in order to prevent Alice's husband being arrested as a hostage; Antigone standing up to the infamous and insignificant French officer who was so shockingly absolved; the role played in her survival, by luck and by friendship—so present in the washroom, in the sharing of the single, tiny blanket, and of her long crawl across the tiled floor of the German hospital to alert her friend Claudine about a forthcoming departure for France. Not to forget the song sung by Rosette with her cut fingers, and the kisses from the dog Gardienne, more human by far than an entire squad of policemen.

All that is missing in these lines is Ida's smile, filled with an understanding sadness that accompanied many of these stories: the adolescent assurance that she didn't cry, the compliments paid by her former teacher, Madame Picard, nurse Wanda's deep sense of compassion, a virtue that the camps appeared to have struck from the list of human attributes. Worth recalling as well are the memorial candles that get placed, every time she visits, in the collapsed ruins of the crematoria; the words "comrade," "buddy," or "girls," repeated with tender gratitude by the eternal "little Ida," whose many talents clearly included making herself loved, and not only by her dog.

It only remains for me to thank the girl, prisoner #75360, for the honor, the privilege, and the enrichment that it was to put together the story of her past over the course of six months, and which never ceased to matter to me.

BERTRAND

You've Got to Tell Them

I have wanted to write this book for a very long time. I thought it was necessary to tell everything that I had seen and lived through myself.

My daughter encouraged me to do it nonstop, but I kept putting it off. I knew that it would be painful to recall some memories that I had buried. When I talk to school kids, I don't talk about everything.

In April 2001, when Wanda passed away before I got a chance to put my arms around her and say the "thank you" that I had held in the bottom of my heart for fifty-six years—the word "thanks" is too weak, but I know of no other—I knew that it was time that I got to work. Fortunately, Bertrand, who had been there when I made my first trip back to the camp and who had also followed Wanda's demise, spontaneously offered to help me. I am very grateful that he understood my intentions and shared my excitement. It is thanks to him that this book was able to see the light of day.

In rereading myself, I am not sure that I insisted enough on the dehumanization in the camps. To be just a number, to possess nothing of one's own except for a metal bowl and a spoon, to be hungry all of the time, always cold in the long winters, to be exhausted, beaten, and fearing the worst all the time. . . . The Jewish women did not have the right to receive mail or packages, of course. We were cut off from the civilized world.

How does one stand up to all of that? I have no answer, unless it is to speak of an incredible lot of lucky breaks. Human nature has some astonishing resources. Not enough to save many of the seventy-six thousand Jews deported from France: only 3 percent would return!

Those of us who did, have a role to play as witnesses. It is for the 97 percent who were murdered that we tirelessly tell our story. Forgetting would be as intolerable as the facts themselves.

After the war, we believed that Nazism and its methods were destroyed forever. When we learned later on of the massacres in Cambodia and in Rwanda, we were forced to admit that the lesson of Auschwitz had not been learned. The Shoah remained a specific tragedy, with its programmed, scientific, and industrial destruction of a people, but it again seemed possible that all those people had died for nothing.

The former deportees viewed the 1948 creation of the state of Israel as an incomparable reassurance; some of them had already been there and taken part in its struggle for independence. Finally, the Jews had a land where they could live as a free people and without persecution, at peace with their neighbors. Hope was reborn. As this event was happening, I thought a lot about my father, who had dreamt of it, and whom the Nazis prevented from experiencing it. The creation of this state was difficult; it still is . . .

If we go and talk to students, it isn't in order for them to have pity on us, but so that they learn what men are capable of doing to other men, for the sole reason that they were born. How such an indoctrination and such propaganda were able to emerge in one of the most civilized peoples in Europe and to lead it to commit such mass crimes? It was indispensable that they first label the Jews as lesser people, and do the same to the Gypsies and the Slavs while they were at it. A plan was in the works to expand Auschwitz and to intern yet more deportees. Without the Allied victories coming from the west and from the east, nobody would have been safe . . .

When one thinks that a million and a half children alone were wiped out! What a loss for humanity! What might they have become?

Once back home, my comrades who got married wanted to have children right away. They saw it as a victory, as getting even for what had happened.

In addition to the Jews themselves, it was their culture that was assassinated. How many Yiddish writers and poets disappeared! How many people are left who speak this language that was so rich and had come down to us across centuries?

Our testimonials are mainly aimed at young people, who welcome them more eagerly than their parents. It took over forty years for people to start teaching the Shoah, for it to appear in history textbooks. The *Association des professeurs d'histoire et de géographie* (Association of Teachers of History and Geography) also managed to get the Second World War moved up in the curriculum so that it falls at the start of the school year and not at the end, where it usually got short shrift. We have the good fortune to live in a republic, in a democracy; young people need to be prepared to protect these freedoms from the temptation of totalitarianism. Because while men are all different, they are completely equal in the eyes of the law. They have the same rights, and their difference enriches each and every one of us.

On the subject of the temptation of totalitarianism, I know of no clearer warning than Rev. Martin Niemoller's, from 1945:

"When the Nazis came to round up the communists, I didn't say anything: I wasn't a communist. When they locked up the Social-Democrats, I didn't say anything: I wasn't a Social-Democrat. When they came to arrest the Jews, I didn't say anything: I wasn't a Jew. When they came for the Catholics, I didn't say anything: I wasn't a Catholic. And when they came to get me, there was nobody left to protest."

I never forget that I received a sacred mission. I can still see the women who entrusted it to me, while they were leaving for the *Revier*, the antechamber of death:

"If you get out, you've got to tell them. They won't believe you, but you've got to tell them."

Them, is you. Today. Tomorrow.

TIME LINE

The Story behind the History

All individual destinies unfold within the context of a group. The dates in our lives all correlate with the dates of everyone else.

Here, in two columns, are Ida's dates, and those of the period she lived through.

IDA	THE REST OF US
1929	
November 19, Ida born in Paris	October 29, Stock Market crashes in New York. Allied occupation of German industrial regions ends. Martin Luther King is born.
1939	
September, first stay in Melle (Deux-Sèvres region)	Germany invades Poland. World War II begins. Sigmund Freud dies.
1940	
June, second stay in Melle begins.	Germany occupies Paris. France surrenders. De Gaulle in London

(continued)

IDA	THE REST OF US
1944	
January 30, Ida is arrested.	The Red Army breaks the siege of Leningrad. The US Army marches on Rome. Joe Frazier is born.
February 10, Ida leaves Drancy for Auschwitz.	The Battle of Anzio in Italy. The Auschwitz. Marshall Islands campaign in the Pacific. Stockard Channing is born.
	June 6, Invasion of Normandy
June 24, Mala's escape	July 20, attempted assassination of A. Hitler by a group of generals
August 22, Mala is hanged.	August 25, Paris is liberated by the Allies (US, Great Britain, France).
	September 7, Vichy government relocated to Germany
October, the revolt of the *Sonderkommandos*	October 10, Soviet army reaches eastern Germany.
1945	
January 7, four women who helped the revolt are hanged.	January 17, Soviet army enters Warsaw.
January 18, Ida on Death March	
January 25, Ida in Ravensbrück	January 25, the Allies win the Battle of the Bulge.
	January 27, Soviets enter Auschwitz.
February 14, Ida in Neustadt until May 3	April 25, US and Soviet armies meet at the Elbe River in Germany.

IDA	THE REST OF US
	1945
	April 30, Hitler commits suicide.
	May 2, Bianca Jagger born
	May 7, Germany surrenders, ending WWII in Europe.
May 30, Ida arrives in hospital in Paris.	May–August, WWII in Pacific continues.
	August 15, Japan accepts Allies' demand that it surrender.
July–September, Ida convalesces in Switzerland.	October 24, United Nations founded in San Francisco

FRENCH PUBLISHER'S AFTERWORD

Ida Grinspan's story account begins on January 31, 1944, and ends in 1945 when she returns to France. The third part, "Then What?," happens now, in our own times, looking back on those dark days.

At the outset of 1944, the war takes a new turn: the Allies' landing in Italy (in September 1943), the Italians' asking for an armistice, and the entry into Rome (in June 1944): the stage is set for a landing in France, which happens on June 6 in Normandy. Certainly, the generals' plot to kill Hitler on July 20 did fail. But the Americans have battled their way across the Pacific, and they liberate Paris on August 25. In December of this year, the Germans' final offensive fails in the Ardennes.

In March of 1945 the Allies cross the Rhine into Germany. They reach Berlin in April. Hitler commits suicide on April 30th. Germany capitulates on May 8th, followed by Japan in August.

SETTING THE STAGE FOR THE HOLOCAUST

At its roots, the word *holocaust* refers to a Jewish religious rite carried out as part of a ceremony of sacrifice during which a victim was burned completely in a fire. In its modern and common use, the term is used today for any extremely large-scale human massacre. When it is written with a capital letter, it makes specific reference to the systematic extermination of European Jewry by the Nazis, which Jews also refer to as the "Shoah."

The Holocaust was set in place by the laws of Nuremberg. This anti-Jewish legislation, announced on September 15, 1935 following a congress of the German National Socialist Party that had been held in the city of Nuremberg, was intended to isolate the Jews "biologically" from the German nation. New laws were passed: those on "Citizenship in the Reich" stripped the Jews of their citizenship and all of their civil rights; those for "the protection of German blood and honor" forbade marriages between Jews and Aryans (ties that had already been contracted were to be dissolved). Sexual relations between Jews and Gentiles were to be punished by a lengthy term in prison. Finally, Jews were no longer allowed to hire German women under the age of forty-five as domestic servants.

In January of 1939, Hitler already considered "the extermination of the Jewish race in Europe" as a probability if war were to break out. After the invasion of Poland in September, the Jews in that country were imprisoned in ghettos where they were obliged to work as forced labor.

In 1940, following the defeat of France, the Nazis briefly considered the possibility of deporting the Jews of Europe to Madagascar, Austria, Czechoslovakia, and Poland. Between spring and fall of 1941, the Nazi leadership took steps to begin the systematic extermination of the Jews:

> —The creation of special mobile SS units organized into task forces (*Einsatzgruppen*) assigned to summarily shoot the leaders and members of the communist party, and all of the Jewish men, women and children, encountered as the German army advanced into Soviet territory.
>
> —The extension of this genocide to the rest of the European continent: the construction of death camps equipped with trucks for gassing people as well as gas chambers using carbon monoxide and then Zyklon B (prussic acid), as well as ovens for cremation.

Finally, on January 20, 1942, the framework for the genocide was finally put in place at a meeting held in a Berlin suburb called Wannsee [pron. VON-say] that was chaired by Heydrich, assisted by Eichmann.[1] Heydrich, the chief of German security services, explained for the first time the nature and scope of the "final solution of the Jewish question" (*Endlösung der Judenfrage*). This enigmatic expression identified the project of exterminating all of the European Israelites or persons deemed to be such by the Nazis.

"Operation Reinhard" was launched in the spring of 1942, with the goal of liquidating the Jews of Poland. The extermination process intensified. Convoys from all over occupied Europe began moving towards the death camps, including Auschwitz-Birkenau.

These concentration camps were, in fact, zones that were cut off from the rest of the world, where people from enemy countries were imprisoned, individuals belonging to ethnic minorities, as well as political prisoners and common criminals. Unlike detention in prisons, where the inmates had been sentenced following a trial, men, women, and children were held in concentration camps for an indeterminate amount of time, without having been judged following a legal process: the people running the camps wield unlimited and arbitrary power. The most common housing in these was in barracks or in tents, surrounded by barbed wire and watchtowers. The concentration camps were sometimes called "reeducation camps," "work camps," "conversion centers," or even "reception centers" by the totalitarian regimes which had set them up.

In 1942, over several months, the Nazis created a vast network intended to funnel their victims into the "triangle of death." Transit camps spread all over occupied Europe were linked by rail to these camps located in the south of Poland in a triangle made up of Treblinka, Chelmno, Sobibor, Belzec, and of course Auschwitz, where the deportees were systematically murdered.

NOTES

FRENCH PUBLISHER'S PREFACE

1. The Poitou is the ancient name of a province in western France, traditionally farm country with many small towns and isolated villages (see Glossary).

FOREWORD, BY IDA GRINSPAN AND BERTRAND POIROT-DELPECH

1. *Le Monde* was one of the two leading daily newspapers in France in 1988.

2. Deux-Sèvres is the name of the French department where Ida was staying (see Glossary).

3. Klaus Barbie, Paul Touvier, and Maurice Papon, three men tried in France in the 1980s and '90s for their roles in World War II France (see Glossary).

PART I: "THE JEWESS OF LIÉ"

1. A Traction Avant is a model Citroën automobile of the period that featured front-wheel drive.

2. Jeune-Lié is a hamlet in the town of Melle, in the Deux-Sèvres department.

3. Normandy is a province in France to the north of Paris, on the English Channel.

4. Ostrów-Mazowiecka (pop. 24,000) is fifty-seven miles northeast of Warsaw (pop. 1.7 million), the capital of Poland.

5. Koprzywnica is a town of 2,500 in the southeast of Poland.

6. *Arrondissement* is the word for an administrative district or zone in Paris.

7. *Pogrom* is a word in Slavic languages for a violent attack on an ethnic or religious group, particularly one aimed at Jews.

8. Clamart is a township on the southwestern outskirts of Paris (see Glossary).

9. Summer of 1942 marks the start of France's intense participation in the Nazi policies of rounding up and deporting undesirables, especially Jews, to death camps in eastern Europe.

10. The Popular Front was a coalition of left-wing political parties that was elected to power in France in 1936. It was out of power by 1938.

11. A *serviette* means a "towel" in French.

12. The Châtelet is a top music and theatrical venue in the center of Paris.

13. The *bois de Vincennes* is a large park on the eastern edge of Paris.

14. Ida's maiden name was Fensterzab, which means "window pane" in Yiddish.

15. A kilometer is roughly six-tenths of a mile, so 30 km is approximately 20 miles.

16. The *Institut d'Histoire du temps présent* (IHTP) is a French history research group at the CNRS (*Centre National de recherches scientifiques*), which sponsored the trip.

17. Pierre Moinot (1920–2007) was a local writer best known for novels and essays.

18. *Wehrmacht* was the traditional German name for its army (see Glossary).

19. The *Rafle du Vel' d'Hiv'* was a roundup of 13,000 Jews in Paris on July 16–17, 1942, named after an indoor bicycle race track where many of the people arrested were detained before they were deported, mostly to Auschwitz.

20. *l'Appel du 18 juin* was a speech given over British Broadcasting by General Charles de Gaulle in response to Philippe Pétain's June 17, 1940 call for an armistice with Germany. De Gaulle asked the French people not to give up the fight.

21. The *gendarmerie* is the French state police, a part of the army, sent from Paris.

22. *Un drôle* is the word for any "guy" in Occitan, and also in Poitevin French. *Une drôlesse* could be translated as a "gal" or perhaps a "chick."

23. Drancy is a town in the northern suburbs of Paris where the French authorities requisitioned an empty apartment complex for use as an internment and transit camp from 1941 to 1944 (see Glossary).

24. A *képi* is the round, flat-topped cap worn by French policemen and army officers.

25. Marshal Philippe Pétain, the head of the French state located in Vichy (see Glossary).

26. *Kommandantur* is the German word for "military headquarters."

27. Karl Oberg and René Bousquet were, respectively, chief of police of the German occupation forces in France and chief of French police forces at this time.

28. TRCP, *Transports en commun de la région Parisienne,* and RATP, *Régie autonome de la région Parisienne,* are names for the Paris mass transit system.

29. Francois Mauriac (1885–1975) was a French novelist and member of the French Academy.

30. Bobigny is the town next to Drancy; the station is about a mile from the camp.

31. Serge Klarsfeld is a French lawyer and activist who has established a list of every convoy and of the names of all of the deportees in them (see Glossary).

32. The Hôpital Broussais is a public facility in the 14th *arrondissement* of Paris.

33. *Gardes mobiles*, or Mobile Guards, were a reserve unit of the French Army.

34. Victor Basch (1863–1944) was a French professor of German thought and a pro-Jewish public intellectual. He and his wife were murdered by Vichy police in Lyon.

35. The CRIF is an organization that grew out of the Jewish resistance movement. Its first aim was to rescue the Jewish community in France from Nazi persecution.

36. The FFI was the result of the fusion of the main bodies of armed resistance.

37. Klaus Barbie was head of the German secret police in Lyon in 1944. In April of that year he ordered the arrest of forty-four Jewish children who were being hidden in a school in nearby Izieu. The children were all deported and murdered by the Nazis.

38. A *maquis* is a kind of resistance group, swollen with young labor-draft resisters. The Glières is a plateau in the Alps in Savoy where a resistance group fought against superior German forces for weeks in early 1944 before being wiped out.

39. The Nazi plan to murder all European Jews was first presented in Wannsee, a suburb of Berlin, in January 1942.

40. The SS (Schützstaffel) was the special militia, which carried out the Nazi Party's anti-Semitic policies both in the field and in the camps (see Glossary).

PART II: FROM A HUMAN TO AN ITEM

1. The station has been preserved to this day (May 31, 2017) (*translator's note*).

2. 2000 km is about 1,240 miles. From Paris to Auschwitz is actually somewhat less than 1,500 km.

3. "Faster! Get out!"

4. Birkenau, also known as Auschwitz II, was built as a combined concentration and death camp starting in October 1941. The older camp, Auschwitz I, two miles away, was thereafter used mainly as a concentration camp for political prisoners.

5. "*Nackt!*" means "Naked!" in German.

6. All references to prisoners in the coming pages use the feminine form of the noun and should be understood as denoting female prisoners (*translator's note*).

7. Ida wrote this in 2002. Her tattoo was still legible in 2017 (*translator's note*).

8. Ida uses the word "*block*" interchangeably with "*barraque*" to designate the buildings in the camp. She also uses the word to denote the residents of such a building (see Glossary).

9. Suzanne Birnbaum, *Une Française juive est revenue*, was first published in 1946 and re-released in 1989 by Herault-Editions.

10. *Revier* [pron. ruh-VEE-er] is the German word for an infirmary. Ida always uses this word, and it is charged with other associations than health care: danger, pain, and death. We have chosen to preserve her use of the word (see Glossary).

11. Upper Silesia is the region of Poland where Auschwitz is situated.

12. German for a "female overseer."

13. A *kommando* [pron. ko-MON-doh] means a work detail. As such it could designate a section of a camp assigned to a job, or a one-time-only group performing a given task. We have chosen to preserve this bit of camp speak as well.

14. Biarritz is a city on the Atlantic Ocean in southwestern France.

15. Clichy is a neighborhood on the north side of Paris, just below Montmartre.

16. Sobibor is the name of a village in eastern Poland where the Nazis built a death camp. Carbon monoxide from a gasoline engine was used to murder about 200,000.

17. Yad Vashem is the official authority in Israel for recognizing and commemorating the Holocaust and also is the name of a museum in Jerusalem run by that authority.

18. Heinrich Himmler was a leading member of the Nazi Party and commander-in-chief of the SS, the German state security forces (see Glossary).

19. General Philippe Leclerc (1902–1947) was a commander in the army that liberated Paris and the north of France. Strasbourg is a French city on the German border.

20. Philippe Pétain (1856–1951) and Pierre Laval (1883–1945) were the leaders of the French government that collaborated with the Nazis during the war (see Glossary).

21. Robert Brasillach was a French journalist who collaborated with the fascists. He was executed for treason on March 31, 1945.

22. Dresden is a large German city that the Allies bombed on February 13–15, 1945.

23. Seventy kilometers is 43 miles.

24. It would appear to have been a railroad hub called Loslau, on the border between the province of Silesia and Moravia (*author's note*).

25. Ravensbrück was a concentration camp for women in Germany, about 60 miles north of Berlin.

26. Neustadt-Glewe is a town in northern Germany. The Nazis had a concentration subcamp there, to which the author is referring.

27. Suzanne and Lea Schwartzman.

28. "Long Live France!"

29. One meter eighty-five to ninety is roughly six feet one to three inches.

30. Two kilometers is about a mile and a half.

31. When the Allied armies defeated the Nazis in 1945, they divided Germany into four Occupation zones, American, British, French, and Soviet Russian. These zones continued to exist.

32. Le Bourget is an airport just north of Paris, France.

33. "Revoir Paris" ("To See Paris Again") is the title of a 1947 song by Charles Trénet.

34. Victor Hugo (1802–1885) is considered the greatest French poet and novelist.

35. *La Marseillaise* is the French national anthem.

36. Thirty kilos is the equivalent of sixty-six pounds.

37. A system for messaging via pneumatic tubes linked post offices across the Paris region from 1879 until 1984.

38. "PX" is a common spoken abbreviation for "Post Exchange."

39. Geneviève de Gaulle, a niece of Gen. Charles de Gaulle, was arrested as a resister and spent three years in Ravensbrück (see Glossary).

40. ADIR stands for *Association nationale des anciennes déportées et internées de la Résistance* (National Association of former deportees and detainees from the Resistance).

41. Montana (now Crans-Montana) is situated in the canton of Valais, Switzerland.

42. Charlotte Delbo, Anise Postel-Vinay née Girard, and Françoise Zavadil were all resisters who had initially been deported to Ravensbrück.

43. The American Jewish Joint Distribution Committee, known familiarly as the Joint, was originally founded in 1914 to aid Jews in Palestine.

44. *Les années noires* is a common euphemism for the years 1940–1944, when France was occupied by the Germans.

45. The *Oeuvre de secours aux enfants* or O.S.E. is a French children's aid organization that was founded in Russia in 1912 and moved to France in 1933. It still exists.

46. *l'Amicale des déportés d'Auschwitz* was founded in 1945 and became the *Union des déportés d'Auschwitz* in 2002.

47. The Quai des Orfèvres is a street in Paris where police headquarters were located.

48. Capital punishment was abolished in France on September 18, 1981.

49. *On the Trail of the Unknown Man*. The book has not been published in English.

50. A *Sous-préfecture* is an office of the French state, located in a town in an area known as a Prefecture. These are administrative areas of the national government.

51. Poirot-Delpech is drawing a parallel with the Greek legend of Antigone, a girl who spoke to power in the person of her brother, Creon, as dramatized by Sophocles.

52. The *Épuration légale* (scholars refer to this as both a legal "Purge" and the "Purification") refers to the period right after World War II (1944–1951), when a High Court prosecuted individuals and organizations in France for war crimes (see Glossary).

53. Nuremberg is the city in Germany where the allies convened an International Military Tribunal (1945–1946) to try the perpetrators of war crimes in World War II.

54. *The Roads to Shame*. The book has not been translated into English.

55. The largest city in the region, Poitiers was the site of a French internment camp. There were internment and transit camps all over the country, but no death camps.

56. The First Statute on the Jews of October 3, 1940 was a decree of the French government stripping Jews of the right to work as doctors, lawyers, and teachers.

57. Miss V. was a teacher who had boarded at Alice's and who knew Ida well.

58. The "Jewish badge" refers to the yellow star, a cloth patch that all Jews in France were required to wear after June 1942.

59. Committees were set up in cities and towns across France starting in December of 1944 to consider issues relative to the liberation of the country that ranged from treason to personal vendettas. This took place independently of the activity of the High Court (*Haute Cour*) (see Glossary).

60. Albert Camus (1913–1960), a leading French author of the day, who signed a petition for clemency in the case of the pro-Nazi writer Robert Brasillach, not because he admired the man or his writings but because Camus opposed the death penalty.

61. Chef Boutonne is the name of a town where Ida could have attended a trade school, but only as a boarding student. Alice thought this would be very risky.

62. *Perdu de vue*, literally "Lost from Sight," a monthly program on French television channel TF1 from 1990 to 1997.

63. An Oflag was a German prisoner-of-war camp reserved for officers.

64. Majdanek was a concentration and extermination camp built by the Nazis near the city of Lublin, Poland.

65. A selection took place whenever the Nazi prison overseers decided to exterminate prisoners deemed unfit for further service.

66. The Association Amicale des Anciens Déportés d'Auschwitz-Birkenau. See www.amicale-des-deportes-auschwitz-et-birkenau-rhone.asso.fr.

67. "Lily Marlene" was a 1939 hit song by Lale Anderson, also sung by Marlene Dietrich. Sometimes called "The Soldier's Song," it was popular throughout World War II.

68. "La Javanaise" (which is also the name of a dance) was a 1968 hit by French songwriter Serge Gainsbourg.

69. La Rochelle is a city of 80,000 on the west coast of France.

70. Laicity, avoidance of explanations or dictates derived from religion.

PART III: THEN WHAT?

1. The World Jewish Congress (WJC) is an organization representing Jews all over the world; see www.worldjewishcongress.org. CRIF is the acronym for the Conseil Représentatif des Institutions Juives de France, at www.crif.org, an organization representing Jewish institutions across France.

2. Free France was the name given to the army in exile that was organized around General Charles de Gaulle in wartime London, and later in Algiers. Its symbol was the Cross of Lorraine.

3. Claude Lanzmann's documentary film *Shoah* premiered in 1985. *Night and Fog*, also a documentary, was made in 1956 by a committee of history teachers for students in the ninth grade, and directed by Alain Resnais. *The Final Stage* is a 1947 Polish film drama set in Auschwitz-Birkenau.

4. Primo Levi (1919–1987) was an Italian survivor of Auschwitz. His book *If this Be a Man* (English title: *Survival in Auschwitz*) is a classic account of survival which sees the guards as well as many of the prisoners as equally devoid of human morality.

5. Liliane Badour was deported to Auschwitz at around the same time as Ida, at age nineteen. Liliane also worked in the *kommando* in the Union Werke factory.

6. Vladimir Jankelevitch (1903–1985) was a Russian-born French scholar who had studied German authors before the war but turned away from support for German culture in any way that he could following the war.

7. In 1979, Kurt Lischka and Herbert Hagen (and a third man, Ernst Heinrichsohn) were accused of committing war crimes while in the security police in France during the war. The three were ultimately convicted and served time in prison.

8. Adolf Eichmann (1906–1962) was a lieutenant colonel charged by the Nazis with organizing the transport of Jews from all over Europe to the death camps. He was tried in Israel for war crimes in 1961 and found guilty. He was hanged in June 1962.

9. Klaus Barbie, a functionary in the Nazi security police who personally tortured prisoners in Lyon, France. He was tried in that city in 1983 and convicted of war crimes and sentenced to life in prison, where he died of cancer (see Glossary).

10. Paul Touvier was a Frenchman who collaborated with the Nazis as head of the Vichy police in the city of Lyon. After many years in hiding, he was tried in 1994. He is the first Frenchman to be tried for crimes against humanity (see Glossary).

11. Maurice Papon was a French civil servant who rose to the rank of minister before being accused of complicity in crimes against humanity for his role in the deportation of Jews from the Bordeaux region (see Glossary).

12. The Annie and Charles Corrin Prize was initiated in France 1989. It recognizes excellence in pedagogy related to the Shoah. It is awarded under the aegis of the *Fonds Social Juif Unifié* and the French ministry of Education.

13. *Schindler's List* (1993) was directed by Steven Spielberg. *Holocaust* is a four-part TV miniseries first broadcast in the United States in 1978. Giancarlo Benigni's *Life is Beautiful* (1997) is a controversial highly awarded comedy-drama set in wartime Italy.

14. René Bousquet (1909–1993) was the chief of French police under the Vichy government. Indicted for crimes against humanity in 1991, he was assassinated at his home in Paris before the trial could begin.

15. Ida's book came out in 2003. Public awareness of, and demand for, witnesses to the deportation from France really took off when President Jacques Chirac made a speech at the anniversary of the Vel' d'Hiv roundup in July 1995. In it he stated unequivocally that France was responsible for what had happened under Vichy.

16. Ida is probably referring to the poem *L'Expiation*, by Victor Hugo, about Napoleon's retreat from Moscow in the winter of 1812.

17. Soviet Gulags refers to similarly brutal prison camps in the Soviet Union.

18. The Hotel Lutétia on the Boulevard Raspail in Paris is where people returning from the camps were brought after they arrived at the Gare de l'Est train station. There they were given aid such as clothing and contact information.

19. The Militia was a paramilitary police force created in January 1943 in Vichy, France (see Glossary). Alain Ferrari's *Milice, film noir* is a 1997 documentary film about it.

20. Poirot-Delpech refers to the trials of Miroslav Radic and Radovan Karadzic.

21. Joseph Stalin (1878–1953) was chief of state in the USSR during World War II. As such he led his country in its heroic fight against the Nazis, but he was also responsible for millions of political arrests and executions of his own opponents.

22. The Cold War is the name given to the global military and economic confrontation between the Western allies and the Soviet Union in the years 1945–1989.

23. For entries by each of these authors, please see the attached Bibliography.

FRENCH PUBLISHER'S AFTERWORD

1. Reinhard Heydrich (1904–1942), an Obergruppenfuhrer in the SS, was chief of Reich Security. Adolf Eichmann (1906–1962), a lieutenant colonel in the SS, was charged with logistics.

GLOSSARY

Note: We have kept some French words in the text in order to preserve the feeling of Ida's speech (e.g., block), as well as some German words where English commonly does the same today (e.g., Reich, Wehrmacht). Since nouns are capitalized in German, we have chosen to keep this convention when using a German word. We have also preserved some words that were particular to the camps (camp speak), but these are not capitalized (e.g., *kapo* and *kommando*).

Barbie, Klaus (1913–1991)—a functionary in the SS when he was named to head the Nazi security forces in Lyon, France in 1942. He was helped by the United States to escape to South America, where he was identified in 1971 thanks to the work of Serge and Beate Klarsfeld. He was later extradited to France for trial.

block—a word in both French and German designating any squarish mass, from paper to architecture, and consequently used by both Ida and Bertrand freely to mean a barrack house as well as the inmates assigned to it.

Clamart—a township in the southwestern suburbs of Paris with approximately 50,000 inhabitants today. It has always been a working-class neighborhood, with many immigrants among its residents.

De Gaulle, General Charles (1890–1970)—fled from France when the government fell into the hands of Philippe Pétain. He went to London and began to organize the Free French in exile. He returned to become president of the Provisional Government in 1945 and was later elected president in the Fifth Republic.

De Gaulle, Geneviève (1920–2002)—detained for acts of resistance, she was a niece of the general and was sent to Ravensbrück by the Nazis. Ida met her during their time spent in Switzerland recovering from deportation. De Gaulle became a spokeswoman for deported Resistance fighters after the war (see Bibliography).

Delbo, Charlotte (1913–1985)—French playwright and political dissident who was deported to Auschwitz for acts of resistance. Ida met her in Switzerland during their time spent recovering from deportation. Delbo's written memoirs are particularly dear to Ida (see Bibliography).

Deux-Sèvres—French administrative district (department) where all of the towns mentioned in connection with Ida's arrest are located. It lies immediately to the west of Poitiers.

Drancy—town in the northern suburbs of Paris where the French authorities requisitioned an empty building for use as an internment and transit camp from 1941 to 1944. It is an apartment complex today, and a museum is there now as well. Most of the 76,000 Jews deported from France passed through it.

Épuration (French)—literally means "Purification"—After the war's end the French provisional government convened a high court to judge people who were accused of charges ranging from high treason to black marketeering. It continued to deliberate until the early 1950s. Many people were stripped of citizenship, disgraced, and barred from work for varying lengths of time. Many were executed.

Himmler, Heinrich (1900–1945)—very early member of the Nazi Party and a close confidant of Adolf Hitler. Himmler commanded the paramilitary organization known as the SS and personally directed the construction and operation of the camps.

Hitler, Adolf (1889–1945)—leader (or *Führer*) of the Nazi Party. He was head of the German state from 1933 until his death.

kapo (camp speak)—a trustee inmate used by the SS, who ran the camps, to control the detainees. According to Germaine Tillion, who was detained in Ravensbrück, *kapos* were mostly recruited from among common criminals.

Klarsfeld, Serge (b. 1935)—French Jewish lawyer who, along with his wife, **Beate**, has spent much of his life documenting the identity of each and every Jewish person deported by the French in World War II (see Bibliography).

kommando (camp speak)—a work detail, a group of people who worked in the same place in the camp.

koya (camp speak)—a bunk bed and/or the people assigned to a particular bunk.

Laval, Pierre (1883–1945)—vice president of the Council of Ministers and later head of government under Philippe Pétain, he was the number two man in the Vichy regime. Starting as a newspaper editor, he was a Socialist and a pacifist, and had even been a prime minister before World War II, but he drifted to the far right. He was executed for treason in 1945.

Milice (la)—The Militia formed in January 1943 in Vichy, France, as the more muscular successor to the *Service d'ordre légionnaire*. The Militia stepped up repression of Jews and non-Jews alike. Pierre Laval was its titular head, but it was in fact energetically led by the previous Vichy security chief, Joseph Darnand.

Papon, Maurice (1910–2007)—a French civil servant in the Ministry of the Interior, Papon did high-level police work from the 1930s into the

1960s. He was successfully tried for the deportation of 1,600 Jews from Bordeaux in 1942 to 1944.

Pétain, Marshal Philippe (1856–1951)—head of the French state during World War II. He was a hero in World War I and had been named a seven-star general, or marshal, following French victory in that conflict. He took power in a constitutional coup d'état in July 1940 and ruled the country from the spa town of Vichy. He was condemned to death for treason but his sentence was commuted to life in prison.

Poitiers—a city in western France (population 44,230 in 1936), 180 miles from Paris. It is the *chef lieu* of the department of Vienne, of the former Poitou-Charentes region, and a subprefecture in today's larger New Aquitaine region.

Poitou (le)—ancient name of the province, to the west of Paris, where Ida was sent to live starting in 1939. It was mostly agricultural at the time, with many medium and small-sized towns and villages. Adjectives: *Poitevin*, *Poitevine*.

Reich (German)—literally means "realm." Nazi Germany called itself the *Grossdeutsches Reich*, the Greater German Reich. Historians often call Nazi Germany the Third Reich, with Bismarck's and Wilhelm's being considered the first and the Weimar Republic the second.

Revier (German)—infirmary, poorly supplied and often staffed with sadists and quack doctors. This word struck terror into the hearts of the already terrorized. In a world where one was only kept alive if one could work, being sent to the infirmary was only slightly better than being selected for execution.

SS (German abbreviation for *Schützstaffel*)—the Nazi Party militia that ran all state security, including the Gestapo, as well as all of the concentration and death camps. All SS men and women had sworn a blood oath of allegiance to Hitler, and were thought to be the country's elite. They were commanded by Heinrich Himmler.

Tilllion, Germaine (1907–2008)—French anthropologist who was detained by the Nazis for acts of resistance and deported to Ravensbrück. After the war, she took an active part in the study of World War II in France and became a spokeswoman for several causes, especially Algerian independence and opposition to torture.

Touvier, Paul (1915–1996)—from a modest background, he grew up in Chambery. He served in the army that was defeated in 1940 but avoided becoming a POW. He drifted into service in the Militia in the Lyon area. He was convicted of crimes against humanity in 1994.

Vichy—a spa town in central France where the government that surrendered to Germany settled in 1940. As such it has become synonymous with the regime that governed the country during the war. (See listing under Pétain, Marshal Philippe.)

Wehrmacht (German)—name given to the German army in World War II.

SELECTED READING

SOME WEBSITES FOR READERS LOOKING FOR MORE INFORMATION:

The Holocaust Education Program Resource Guide, http://www.holocaust-trc.org/the-holocaust-education-program-resource-guide/holocaust-bibliography/.

http://motlc.wiesenthal.com/site/pp.asp?c=gvKVLcMVIuG&b=394709.

Suggested Bibliography—The Holocaust—Yad Vashem, http://www.yadvashem.org/yv/en/holocaust/resource_center/bibliography.asp

INTERESTED READERS SHOULD ALSO EXPLORE THE RESOURCES OF THE UNITED STATES HOLOCAUST MEMORIAL MUSEUM:

https://www.ushmm.org/

OTHER SOURCES OF INTEREST, INCLUDING ONES BY PEOPLE MENTIONED IN IDA AND BERTRAND'S TEXT:

Azéma, Jean-Pierre. *From Munich to the Liberation, 1938–1944*. Cambridge, UK: Cambridge University Press, 1985.

Berger, Alvin H. *The End of the Holocaust*. Bloomington, IN: Indiana University Press, 2013.

de Gaulle-Anthonioz, Geneviève. *The Dawn of Hope: A Memoir of Ravensbrück*. New York: Arcade, 1999.

Delbo, Charlotte. *Auschwitz and After*. New Haven, CT: Yale University Press, 1997. (Includes the text of three books: *None of Us Will Return; Useless Knowledge; Days and Memory.*

———. *Convoy to Auschwitz: Women of the French Resistance*. Boston, MA: Northeastern University Press, 1997.

Jeanneney, Jean-Noël. *Une histoire des médias, des origines à nos jours*. Paris: Points, 1990.

Levi, Primo. *Survival in Auschwitz*. New York: Barnes & Noble, 2013.

Moorehead, Caroline. *A Train in Winter: An Extraordinary Story of Women, Friendship, and Resistance in Occupied France*. New York: HarperCollins, 2011.

———. *Village of Secrets: Defying the Nazis in Vichy France*. New York: HarperCollins, 2014.

Rémond, René. *Paul Touvier et l'Eglise*. In collaboration. Paris: Fayard, 1992.

Ricoeur, Paul. *Memory, History, Forgetting*. Chicago, IL: University of Chicago Press, 2004.

Rousso, Henry. *The Vichy Syndrome: History and Memory in France since 1944*. Cambridge, MA: Harvard University Press, 1994.

Tillion, Germaine, *Ravensbrück*. Garden City, NY: Doubleday, 1975.

Vidal-Naquet, Pierre. *Assassins of Memory: Essays on the Denial of the Holocaust*. New York: Columbia University Press, 1993.